THE
REFERENCE
SHELF

U.S.
DEFENSE
POLICY

edited by CHRISTOPHER A. KOJM

THE REFERENCE SHELF
Volume 54 Number 2

THE H. W. WILSON COMPANY

New York   1982

THE REFERENCE SHELF

The books in this series contain reprints of articles, excerpts from books, and addresses on current issues and social trends in the United States and other countries. There are six separately bound numbers in each volume, all of which are generally published in the same calendar year. One number is a collection of recent speeches; each of the others is devoted to a single subject and gives background information and discussion from various points of view, concluding with a comprehensive bibliography. Books in the series may be purchased individually or on subscription.

Library of Congress Cataloging in Publication Data

Main entry under title:

U.S. defense policy.
    (The Reference shelf; v. 54, no. 2)
    Bibliography: p.
    1. United States—Military policy—Addresses, essays, lectures.
I. Kojm, Christopher A.   II. Title: US defense policy.
III. Series.
UA23.U17   355'.0335'73   82-2631
ISBN 0-8242-0666-5   AACR2

PRINTED IN THE UNITED STATES OF AMERICA

CONTENTS

3

III.   U.S. CONVENTIONAL FORCES

IV.   DOLLARS AND SENSE

PREFACE

In fulfillment of his election campaign promises, President Ronald Reagan in March 1981 outlined plans for huge increases in the defense budget. His administration requested $1.3 trillion in defense spending over the next five years; $200 billion more than the sum proposed by the Carter administration in its ambitious five-year program to increase military expenditure.

Although committed to deep cuts in domestic spending, the Reagan administration planned to increase the defense budget because of its conviction that the United States has failed to match the steady buildup of Soviet military power. According to President Reagan, only a major U.S. defense effort can check the Soviet Union in its drive toward world domination.

Not all, however, shared the President's views. Many claim that his administration lacks a clear foreign policy and a well-defined defense strategy, and that Reagan's military bravado seems to frighten allies of the United States more than it impresses the Soviet Union. Some believe that the likely consequence of increased defense spending is another round in the superpower arms race rather than the restoration of U.S. military superiority. It is also feared that massive military spending may cause a shortage of engineers and raw materials, and drive up prices instead of improving the nation's security.

Some of those who enthusiastically endorse a boost in defense spending are critical of the administration's priorities. Are we pursuing a foreign policy that coordinates political goals with military strategies and the structure of our armed forces? Are we purchasing the right kind of weaponry for the 1980s? Are U.S. forces ready to go to war if called upon? Are we getting the most out of our defense dollars?

These are some of the questions addressed by this compi-

lation. Section I places the question of defense in the context
of U.S. foreign policy: what is the nature of security, and what
is achieved by maintaining a well-armed and prepared military? Section II examines the nuclear modernization program
proposed by President Reagan in October 1981 and discusses
arms control. Section III looks at U.S. conventional forces, including the all-volunteer army and the future of the U.S.
Navy. It examines the commitments proclaimed by President
Carter and echoed by President Reagan to defend U.S. interests in the Persian Gulf. Section III also asks whether we are
buying the right kind of weapons: are they becoming too expensive, too fragile and too sophisticated for the rugged requirements of the battlefield? Finally, Section IV examines
dollars and sense. Can we afford President Reagan's defense
budget? On the other hand, can we afford not to increase our
defenses? Are we spending defense dollars effectively, or indeed, as a new school of military reformers would ask, are we
even posing the right questions?

The compiler wishes to thank Nancy Hoepli, Ann Mis-
back, Bruce Carrick and the many authors and publishers
who have courteously granted permission to reprint their materials in this book.

CHRISTOPHER A. KOJM

January 1982

I. STRATEGIES OF NATIONAL SECURITY

EDITOR'S INTRODUCTION

Military budgets and military priorities are ultimately determined by our perceptions of the world and the dangers beyond the borders of the United States. Will the United States be in a position of unprecedented vulnerability during the 1980s, or are our defenses strong, and our strategic position preferable to that of any other nation? As the first article, written by the editor of this compilation, points out, national security cannot be defined by military terms alone; it also has political, economic and diplomatic dimensions. In order to understand the problems of U.S. security, it is useful to trace the origins of the nation's vast military commitments.

The second article, a speech by Edmund S. Muskie, President Carter's Secretary of State, is the Carter administration's account of its defense record. Muskie notes the military improvement programs which the Carter administration began and expanded. He also explains the Carter administration's basis for cautious optimism: the Soviet Union faces far worse problems, and arms control agreements—particularly the SALT II treaty—can offer a significant contribution to U.S. security.

The third article, a speech by Secretary of Defense Caspar W. Weinberger, details the Reagan administration's conception of the threats to U.S. security. The Soviet Union has vastly increased its armaments, and has shown itself willing to use them for its own imperial ends. The United States, in contrast, became complacent during the decade of détente, failing to make the military efforts necessary to maintain a global balance of power.

In the final article in this section Seymour Melman offers radical criticism of the military policies of both superpowers. The superpowers strive to build stronger, faster, smarter and deadlier weapons, but both fail to realize that nuclear overkill and guerrilla warfare place strict limits on the usefulness of

7

both nuclear and conventional power. If weapons cannot achieve political ends, of what use are weapons?

AMERICA'S DEFENSE: A SHORT HISTORY[1]

It can no longer be seriously denied that the overall military balance is shifting sharply against us. . . . Whatever the causes, unless current trends are reversed, the 1980s will be a period of vulnerability such as we have not experienced since the early days of the Republic.

Henry A. Kissinger, 1980

America's military strength is formidable. I know of no responsible military official who would exchange our strategic position for that of any other nation.

Cyrus R. Vance, 1979

Two former secretaries of state, the leading spokesmen on foreign policy for three American presidents, offered these strikingly different assessments of America's military strength. And in the 1980 presidential campaign, the issue of whether America was militarily second rate—or second to none—was debated with singular passion. Candidate Ronald Reagan charged that "America's defense strength is at its lowest ebb . . . in both strategic and conventional arms." President Jimmy Carter's Secretary of Defense, Harold Brown, countered: "I believe that those who mistakenly claim that the United States is weak or that the Soviet Union is strong enough to run all over us are not only playing fast and loose with the truth, they are also playing fast and loose with U.S. security."

What Is Security?

The security of the United States, or for that matter of any other country, cannot be defined in military terms alone. Se-

---

[1] Excerpt from *The ABC's of Defense: America's Military in the 1980s*, by Christopher A. Kojm, senior editor, and the editors of the Foreign Policy Association. Headline Series 254, Ap. '81. p 4–10. Copyright © 1981 The Foreign Policy Association, Inc. Reprinted by permission.

curity has economic, political and diplomatic dimensions which military force can supplement but cannot supplant. The key elements at home are a strong economy, effective leadership, and a consensus on foreign policy goals. Abroad, they include stable relations with our allies in Europe and Japan and with our neighbors in the Western Hemisphere. The important issues of resources and markets, trade and finance will require careful and continuous U.S. negotiations with both the developed and developing countries; they are questions rarely susceptible to military answers. More-traditional notions of security, however, focus on the nature of military threats—and the kind and degree of U.S. response.

A wise foreign policy tailors the level of national commitment and expenditure to the size of the interests which are at stake. A diplomatic protest, which costs little, is adequate in some instances; economic aid can be adjusted to meet a specific need, from a few thousand dollars to set up a school in a developing country to the billions in aid which the United States spends annually to underwrite the Egyptian-Israeli peace treaty. Economic sanctions, such as the [1980–81] grain embargo of the Soviet Union, cost some groups (farmers) more than others. A demonstration of military power may not cost much: the United States can exert influence through military sales, Navy port calls, or by sending AWACS (airborne warning and control system) radar planes to help a friend. But a military pledge can also lead to a whole new level of commitment, from a simple "pledge to consult" to a pledge to shed blood, if necessary, to defend U.S. allies or interests.

The Prussian General Clausewitz called war "a continuation of politics by other means." Throughout history, force has been exercised for political goals. But because it costs so much in both blood and treasure, most great powers have preferred to exercise the *threat* of force rather than force itself to deter attack or defend their interests.

According to the axiom "the sword in the scabbard is in use," a strong military force acts to deter potential adversaries from provoking conflict. The threat of force works well as a political tool so long as others believe that the threat will be exercised. By the same token, the deterrence of attack by an adversary rests upon the *credibility* of one's own military force (Is it strong enough? Does my adversary believe that I will use it?) and a clear, if tacit, definition of what one would defend with force—lest war come about through miscalculation.

Few would disagree that the best conceivable outcome of any dispute would be to achieve one's aims without war, and that military superiority—or what the adversary perceives as superiority—helps to achieve this. But if war does break out, its course is uncertain. Once war begins, it assumes a logic of its own. In 1914 the great powers stumbled into a war which none wanted and which all assumed would be over in a matter of weeks; instead the war continued for four years, with tragic consequences. Even when military force is applied in a popular cause, as in World War II, it can lead to tremendous sacrifice. With the advent of nuclear weapons, the use of force has become not only infinitely more dangerous but also more unpredictable. In democratic countries, the use of military force is generally threatened only when there exists a broad consensus that "vital interests" are endangered—interests over which the nation is truly prepared to go to war.

America's Interests: Which Are Vital?

Nations try to maintain—and if possible augment—their political power, influence and economic position. They tend to define their vital interests according to what they think they can afford. As the United States grew in wealth and power in the 19th and 20th centuries, the number of its vital interests increased.

Clearly today the United States would use armed force to deter or defend itself against direct attack, either conventional or nuclear. A second and closely related vital interest is to secure U.S. borders. Canada is one of our closest allies; Mexico, while deeply ambivalent about the "North Americans," has generally friendly and mutually advantageous ties with the United States. In any event, Mexico represents no military threat. Elsewhere in the Americas, the United States, since its defeat of Spain in 1898, has possessed the means to

uphold the Monroe Doctrine and limit the influence of outside powers in the Western Hemisphere. While the Caribbean is no longer solely "an American lake," the United
States remains militarily preponderant in the region.

In the wake of two world wars, the vital interests of the
United States expanded as it assumed the mantle of world
leadership. In Europe, the United States, like England in previous centuries, sought to maintain the balance of power. To
prevent Germany from dominating Europe, the United States
went to war in 1917 and again in 1941. When victory was
achieved and the balance of power apparently restored in
1918 and 1945, the United States rushed to demobilize and
bring its troops home. But a new challenge in Europe after
World War II—the perceived threat of Communist aggression and subversion directed by Moscow—led the United
States to forge the North Atlantic Treaty Organization
(NATO) and return its forces, this time to a friendly Germany.

In the Far East, the United States went to war in 1941 to
prevent Japan from dominating the Pacific basin. America
emerged triumphant and sent its forces to occupy and help
rebuild Japan (as it did Germany) in its democratic image.
Japan became an American ally—and its security and stability, vital U.S. interests.

When Communist North Korea attacked South Korea in
1950, the United States belatedly decided that South Korea,
too, fell within the U.S. Pacific security perimeter. U.S. troops
fought there under the United Nations banner. South Korea's
defense, important in its own right, was perhaps just as important as a symbol of U.S. credibility to Japan. In Europe,
Berlin served as a similar touchstone of U.S. military resolve,
particularly to Germany. In addition to its security pledge to
Europe and Japan, the United States undertook to keep the
air and sea lanes of the Atlantic and Pacific open, lanes vital
for trade in peacetime and for military resupply of allies in
time of war.

In the postwar era America seemed omnipotent. Shocks in
Asia led it to extend still further its commitments and military
forces. The victory of Communist forces in China in 1949 and

the defeat of France in Indochina in 1954 were perceived as triumphs for the Soviet Union and international communism. In response, the United States in 1954 pressed for the creation of the Southeast Asia Treaty Organization (SEATO), designed as an Asian parallel to NATO. That same year the United States signed a mutual defense treaty with the Chinese Nationalist regime in Taiwan.

Three presidents justified growing U.S. involvement in South Vietnam on America's SEATO obligations. John F. Kennedy introduced the first military advisers in 1961, Lyndon B. Johnson sent ground troops in 1965, and by 1968 the United States had committed over half a million men. But the military effort failed to stabilize South Vietnam and caused deep political division at home. With pain, the United States discovered for the first time that its security commitments exceeded its willingness to expend its resources. President Richard M. Nixon and Assistant to the President for National Security Affairs Henry Kissinger sought to extricate the U.S. forces in a way that, at a minimum, provided a decent interval before the collapse of South Vietnam, leaving U.S. defense commitments elsewhere in the world intact.

After the fall of South Vietnam in April 1975, SEATO quietly disbanded. By then the process of normalizing relations with the People's Republic of China was under way, and much of the rationale for fighting international communism in Asia had seemingly evaporated. No one seriously spoke of the reintroduction of U.S. ground forces in Southeast Asia, and in 1979 the United States abrogated its defense treaty with Taiwan. Both Taiwan and the members of the Association of Southeast Asian Nations (Indonesia, Malaysia, Philippines, Singapore and Thailand) continued to receive U.S. political support and military aid. But they were expected to provide for their own defense.

The Middle East

In the Middle East, as in Europe and Asia, the United States attempted to organize a defense perimeter to halt the advance of international communism. The Central Treaty Organization, which grew out of the Baghdad Pact, was formed in 1959. Members included Turkey, Pakistan, Iran and Britain, with the United States a "participating non-member." When Britain, the traditional military protector, withdrew its forces from the Persian Gulf in 1971, President Nixon tried to shore up the shah of Iran as the new protector of Western interests. After the oil embargo and oil price hikes of 1973–74 starkly illustrated the dependence of the industrial democracies on Middle East producers, the United States decided to let the shah buy whatever weapons he thought he needed to protect the Gulf.

The shah of Iran tumbled from power in January 1979, and with him fell U.S. influence. The seizure of U.S. diplomatic personnel as hostages in Teheran in November 1979 and the December 1979 Soviet invasion of Afghanistan left Americans angry, frustrated and feeling terribly vulnerable to events in the Middle East which seemed beyond their control. In January 1980 President Carter announced that the United States would now act directly in the region to protect its interests: "An attempt by any outside force to gain control of the Persian Gulf region will be regarded as an assault on the vital interests of the United States of America. And such an assault will be repelled by any means necessary, including military force." To defend the Gulf, the Carter Administration drew up plans for a Rapid Deployment Force (RDF) for possible intervention in the region. The newly minted "Carter Doctrine," in contrast to the U.S. commitments to NATO and Japan, has yet to achieve general acceptance.

But even the inherited wisdom of past Administrations is not immune, on occasion, to questioning. A school of isolationists, tracing its origins to George Washington's "Farewell Address," asks if our commitment to Europe and Japan is not too much. A second school of global interventionists believes that our commitment is too little: does not Soviet-inspired radical change in the third world call for a greater American military response? Isolationists are criticized for their complacent willingness to abjure America's leadership role;

interventionists are criticized for their strident unwillingness
to recognize the limits of American power.

U.S. Military Personnel in Foreign Areas (In thousands, rounded off)					
	1964	1968	1972	1976	1980
Germany	263	225	210	213	244
Other Europe	119	66	62	61	65
Europe, Afloat	54	23	26	41	22
South Korea	63	67	41	39	39
Japan and Ryukyus	89	79	64	45	46
Other Pacific	27	37	25	27	15
Pacific, Afloat (including Southeast Asia)	52	94	51	24	15
Thailand	4	48	47	1	—
South Vietnam	16	534	47	—	—
Miscellaneous Foreign	68	27	22	8	42
Total	755	1,200	595	460	489

Source: *Department of Defense Annual Report FY 1982*

Schools of strategic thought contend. One of the key issues
is whether current U.S. strategy, which calls for sufficient
forces to fight "one-and-one-half wars"—a "major" war in
either Europe or the Pacific and a "minor" war in the Persian
Gulf or elsewhere in the third world—is adequate for the
1980s.

ESSENTIALS OF SECURITY: ARMS AND MORE[2]

In recent months the atmosphere has been unusually thick
with pronouncements about an American military decline.
We cannot let such funereal forecasts go unanswered. They
are wrong on the facts, and they can be dangerous in their effect.

I am here today to take sharp issue with the evangelists of

[2] Reprint of an address by Edmund S. Muskie, President Carter's Secretary of
State, before the World Affairs Council in Pittsburgh on September 18, 1980. *Department of State Bulletin.* 80:27–8. N. '80.

American weakness—to affirm that America today is strong and growing stronger. If our nation truly was neglecting its defenses, it would be the duty of all informed people to sound the alarm. But false declarations of weakness only intensify the dangers we face. They can cause our friends to doubt us and our enemies to discount us. They can distract us from other work necessary to make our society stronger and our world more secure.

The Defense Record

So let us evaluate the defense record, but let us evaluate it fairly. Let us weigh the East-West balance realistically. And let us give due regard to our own strength as well as that of our opposition.

Our allies are stronger, our alliances sturdier than those of the Soviet Union. In economic power, the United States and our NATO allies outstrip the Warsaw Pact more than two to one. Taken together, we devote more to defense than the Warsaw Pact, including the Soviet Union. Our alliances have the added dependability that is derived when values and purposes are truly shared. Unlike the Warsaw Pact, NATO members and Japan are allies by choice. The purpose of our alliances is not to camouflage the ambitions of one member but to defend the freedom of all.

At least one-fourth of the Soviet Union's ground combat forces are tied down on the long common border with China. The nations on our borders are friends.

Technology is another American advantage. "Faster," "more accurate," "more advanced"—these generally are terms that apply to American weapons and American systems. Soviet technology has lagged behind.

And our security is also advanced by the content of our foreign policy—by the international principles we support. On a global basis, we stand for essential precepts of national sovereignty and human rights. Certainly we live in a tumultuous world, characterized by the unremitting nationalism and surging human aspirations of more than 100 new nations. But if such an environment is unsettling to us, it will prove to be even more perilous for nations seeking to dominate others and dictate their systems. Such imperial concepts are the wave of the past. They collide head-on with the historic trends now underway virtually everywhere in the world— from the patriots in Afghanistan to the nationalists in every nation of the Third World, from the democratic forces in Zimbabwe to the gallant workers of Poland who have inspired us all.

In sum, our technology, our solid security partnerships, our identification with national independence and human freedom—all of these assets should strengthen our confidence as we assess the sufficiency of our defenses.

They do not, however, give us cause for complacency. Our military posture continues to require our diligent attention. In the Soviet Union, we face a rival that has engaged for more than a generation in a steady buildup of its military forces, both conventional and strategic. In strategic nuclear forces the Soviets have attained a rough equivalence. In the conventional area they have increased the danger to our Asian and European allies. They have aimed for the status of global power—the capacity for direct involvement even in distant regions. And now in Afghanistan they have shown no hesitancy in applying their power in a brutal attempt to crush a sovereign neighbor.

The question facing Americans is not whether we should respond to these developments; all agree that we must. The real question is whether we will continue with a well-conceived and measured response tailored to the actual threats we face or whether we will run off wildly in all directions at once, spending vastly greater sums to little, if any, effect.

Let me briefly survey what the response thus far has been. In overall terms our arms spending is no longer dropping. It is growing. Our defense spending declined in 7 of the 8 years just before President Carter took office—a total drop of more than 37%.

Since President Carter's inauguration, however, defense spending has increased 4 years in a row—for overall growth of 10% after inflation. And if the President's 5-year plan is carried out, the increase by 1985 will exceed 27%.

To make it absolutely clear that we are not proposing to squeeze our Armed Forces, let me just note here that this 5-year defense program calls for appropriations of over $1 *trillion* between now and 1985.

Even so, there are those who pronounce that effort insufficient. They insist upon a still larger arms budget. They will not tell us what it would contain. They leave those decisions for later. They simply want "more"—of whatever, as if shoveling out the taxpayer's money is a desirable end in itself. That is a formula not for greater security but for guaranteed waste—a failing to avoid in defense just as much as in any other part of the budget.

Instead we need a carefully structured defense program that responds effectively to specific dangers. And that is what we have. In conventional forces, the Carter Adminstration began promptly in 1977 to address the military deficiencies of NATO—matters which previously had received abundant discussion and precious little concrete attention.

Today the NATO Long-Term Defense Program, an American initiative, is in its third year. Problems ranging from readiness and prompt reinforcement to integrating air defenses are no longer simply being studied; they are being solved. These NATO improvements are underwritten by an alliance agreement to increase defense spending by at least 3% each year—another initiative of the United States.

We are engaged in a broad modernization of the Army's weapons and equipment. We have begun the first full-scale modernization of tactical air forces since the Vietnam war. And our shipbuilding program will produce 97 new ships over the next 5 years, building toward a newer and more capable fleet of 550 ships, in contrast to 476 in 1977.

With these programs moving forward, we have also begun bolstering our ability to respond to emergencies outside the major alliance regions—including the vital Middle East-Persian Gulf area. Our naval presence there today is the strongest ever. We have negotiated new agreements for access to ports and airfields. We are prepositioning equipment and supplies in the Indian Ocean area. A new cargo aircraft is being developed. The elements of a rapid deployment force have been designated, and exercises are underway.

Our programs in the area of nuclear weapons reflect this same commitment to the deterrence of war through the assurance of strength. Last year, NATO adopted our recommendations for modernizing theater nuclear forces in Europe. On intercontinental or stategic nuclear forces, the hard decisions have been made. A sweeping modernization of all three parts of our nuclear triad—land, sea, and air—is moving ahead.

• For the strategic bomber forces, President Carter took the soundest course, even though it meant also taking some political heat. Instead of sinking billions of dollars in a B-1 bomber with a doubtful future, he decided to equip our existing bombers with air-launched cruise missiles. In place of an old concept highly vulnerable to Soviet countermoves, he selected an array of advanced technologies that can surmount foreseeable Soviet defenses.

• At sea, the Trident submarine program was put back on track. The first of those modern submarines will join the fleet next year. Portions of the existing fleet already have the Trident I missile, with major improvements in range and power.

• And on the land, the new MX missile, with mobile basing, will overcome the chief source of potential nuclear instability—the growing vulnerability of missiles fixed in silos. As with our bomber forces, President Carter rejected second-best suggestions and made sure we had the best plan before construction began, so we would not have to waste time and money later fixing the mistakes.

SALT II

Along with these programs—cruise missiles, Trident, the MX—there is a fourth program I want to mention—a "secret weapon," if you will. Let me list some of its capabilities. By itself, this secret weapon would knock out about one-fourth of all long-range Soviet missiles and bombers that we project for

1985. It would do that without launching a nuclear war; indeed, without even firing a shot. In the process, it would eliminate thousands of individual warheads and bombs that the Soviet arsenal could otherwise have aimed at our country. The secret weapon has surveillance capabilities. With it, we will be able to keep better track of Soviet forces and programs.

For all of its military effectiveness, there is no incompatibility whatsoever between this secret weapon and our other strategic programs. MX, Trident, and air-launched cruise missiles can all go ahead as planned. Adding this weapon will not require massive new appropriations. In fact, in the long run, money will be saved. Nor does it worry our allies. On the contrary, they know about it, and they strongly support it. Their only concern is that we might not adopt it.

Of course the weapon I am referring to is not a weapon at all. It is an agreement—the SALT II Treaty. But it, nonetheless, will make all the contributions to our security I have just described. There is nothing soft or innocent about it. It is an integral part of a hard-headed strategy of American defense. And it should be recognized as such. Indeed, it may well be that some of those who oppose SALT II would support it— even insist on it—if it were a defense expenditure that could buy the same results.

The contribution of SALT to our defense underscores the second of two messages I want to leave here today. The first, as I have suggested, is that our defenses—alone and in combination with our allies—are second to none. We are determined to see that they remain so. That determination is not just stated in words; it is backed up in the budget. The second message is that simply spending more money and building more arms—even accumulating vast military power—will not be enough to assure our security in today's world.

Enhancing U.S. Security

Even our defense posture itself depends upon other international assets and skills. Recall NATO's Long-Term Defense

Program, its agreement on greater defense efforts, the decision on theater nuclear forces, our access to facilities in the Indian Ocean. Actions such as these cannot be manufactured out of either unilateral announcements or unspecified new spending. They are the products of careful negotiation and steady leadership—endeavors every bit as vital to our defense as arms.

And those endeavors have other applications indispensable to our security. True security in a nuclear age demands steps that lessen the risk that war will happen. That is the mandate of arms control—in combination with a strong defense, to help achieve a stable balance and to avoid miscalculation by either side. For we know that nuclear war would mean catastrophe for every side. In such times it would only jeopardize our security to reject arms control and embrace doctrines—including the chimera of nuclear superiority—that invite a nuclear arms race.

Our security is also advanced by a vigorous diplomacy—fashioning a mature, stable basis of cooperation even with countries, such as China, that have different systems from ours. We must not retreat from those efforts, confuse them, or be confused by them.

Our security has been enhanced by the success of peacemaking in Zimbabwe. That effort deprived our adversaries of a conflict to exploit. Some Americans wanted to disrupt the peace process by prematurely ending our participation in international sanctions. We can all be grateful they did not prevail.

Our security is still more deeply involved in the Middle East, where the Camp David process has produced the first real peace agreement since Israel came into being. Only patient, persistent, and imaginative diplomacy can reconcile the remaining issues—the same kind of diplomacy that hammered out the accords at Camp David. Bellicose pronouncements or assaults on the negotiating process that offer no concrete alternatives neither advance that enterprise nor serve the cause of peace.

And our security is affected by a broad range of economic

issues that arms cannnot touch. We could never have blasted a new trade agreement into being. We cannot threaten stagnating economies to make them prosper or intimidate hungry people into health.

Yet our fate ultimately turns on such questions, even as it rests on the balance of power. If we neglect such challenges, our fate may be to slide into oblivion, rather than being blown there. But we will get there all the same.

In short, our security in the future requires the same priorities that have marked our foreign policy in the recent past. On defense, we must continue the steady, prudent improvement of our Armed Forces. We must specifically repudiate the false message that ours is a frail nation. And our security requires something more. It requires a realistic understanding of the nature of the world we share, a commitment to peace as well as power; a capacity to work constructively with others to advance common purposes and meet the full range of challenges ahead.

I am convinced that the American people understand the need for such a balanced American approach to the world. I believe they support a defense posture of strength and confidence and a foreign policy of construction and hope.

REQUIREMENTS OF OUR DEFENSE POLICY[3]

... Our defense policy must be comprehensive and cover many aspects of our security. It must enable us to cope with all the significant threats, with all the plausible contingencies that might endanger our security. When it comes to the security of our country, we cannot prepare for only those threats that are easy to handle. In the final analysis our ultimate goal is to do everything necessary to preserve peace with freedom and to do it in time. ... Peace alone is not enough. Poland is technically at peace. We must secure peace with freedom,

[3] Reprint of an address by Caspar W. Weinberger, Secretary of Defense, before the United Press International (UPI) luncheon of the American Newspaper Publishers Association in Chicago on May 5, 1981. *Department of State Bulletin.* 80:46–8. Jl. '81.

not only for today but for the future; not only for ourselves and our descendants, but for those many other nations which have joined us in an alliance for the common defense.

From our alliance commitments stem some important constants for our strategy, tactics, and deployment, because these matters have been arranged by common agreement. And if, because of a growing threat or new technology change is needed, we will again seek common agreement to bring it about.

Thus, among the constants of our defense policy, is the agreed basic strategy for NATO, which requires strong conventional, theater nuclear, and strategic nuclear forces to provide the full spectrum of deterrence. We are also recommitted to strengthen U.S. conventional forces in Europe, to improve their readiness, and to move forward with the agreed modernization of theater nuclear weapons and our associated effort at arms control negotiations.

Changes in Policy

What has changed in our determination to respond realistically to the growing threats wherever they confront our national security? For well over a decade, the Soviet Union's spending on conventional armaments has been about double our own. And its investment in strategic nuclear armaments has been triple that of the United States. These facts aren't new; you have heard them before.

What is new is that Americans, last fall [1980], reasserted their belief that our nation must restore its military strength as President Reagan promised. What is new is that we have decided that America can, and in fact must, remain a great power if we are to keep peace and freedom. What is new is the determination of President Reagan, and those of us who serve him, to cut back Federal spending and reduce the role of government, thereby making room for a vigorous expansion in our defense effort, without causing more inflation.

The Soviet buildup in armaments over the last 15 years is not the only changed threat we must address. During the same period, Soviet power has been growing in other important ways. The Soviet Union has greatly extended its geostrategic reach by establishing military outposts in the Middle East, in Africa, and elsewhere. Soviet footholds in Ethiopia, Yemen, and Afghanistan threaten the vital oilfields of the Middle East and, indeed, the peace of the world. These bases and facilities were formerly neutral or accessible to us. And Soviet forces have increasingly been designed and deployed to take advantage of this farflung access they have gained.

As Soviet ability to project its power abroad has grown, American and allied access to bases and airspace has declined in many areas of critical concern, particularly in the vital regions of the Middle East. During this same period, we have let our strategic superiority be eroded. We have long tolerated this deterioration in our relative nuclear strength because we hoped that the nuclear balance could be stabilized through arms control agreements and that the Soviet leadership, in fact, shared our goal for such a stable nuclear balance.

It is an unfortunate, indeed, a tragic, fact that this hope of ours has been badly disappointed—the Soviet expenditures for armaments, in particular strategic arms, grew more rapidly and more steadily during the period called détente than during the so-called cold war. This is not to say détente caused the Soviet buildup, as some European journalists felt I have said. It is to say that détente slowed only our investment in strategic arms.

As I am stressing the need to respond to the relentless growth in Soviet arsenals, I do not want to be misunderstood to mean that Soviet military power is the only threat of concern to the Defense Department. We and our allies have come to be critically dependent on places in the world which are subject to great instability. Many of our vital resources come from such areas in the world. And in those areas, some nations are both strongly armed and hostile toward us. These local threats to our interest, and local instabilities, in general, often present a temptation to various forms of Soviet intervention. They constitute the troubled waters that are a favorite fishing ground of the Soviets. We need only to look at

Syria, Iran, and Iraq, to say nothing of the Caribbean disturbances, to see this.

We cannot meet alone all the farflung challenges that may arise. We have to count on increased and closer cooperation with our friends and allies. Indeed, the commitments and interests that we are bound to support in almost every quarter of the globe are not isolated points of concern. For example, what we do to assure uninterrupted access to oil from the Persian Gulf affects Japan and Israel and all our European allies. What Japan does to strengthen its defense enhances our ability to fulfill our treaty obligations to Australia and New Zealand. What Australia and New Zealand contribute to safeguarding the eastern approaches to the Indian Ocean increases our capabilities and NATO's to counter any coercive threats on NATO's distant flanks—Turkey and Norway. Our interests and commitments, our alliances and our treaties, are both obligations and assets at once.

This interlock of interests and commitments of the free world creates mutual obligations to share in the burdens of our common defense. I believe President Reagan set an example of courage and political leadership by trimming back sharply many domestic government expenditures with large constituencies, while expanding our resources needed to meet the growing military threat. I know our allies have been deeply impressed by this example. I hope that many of them will find it possible to follow it. As partners in the common defense, we must all assume an appropriate effort at appropriate levels.

In the past, we and our allies enjoyed a commanding lead in technology and its defense applications. Today we cannot take for granted that this lead exists and will be maintained in matters important for our defense. I am confident that the United States has the human resources to hold and keep that lead—the skills, the imagination, the ingenuity. But we have not sufficiently viewed our technology as a valuable, and limited, national resource, and we neglected that part of this resource which must be devoted to keeping our nation strong and free. We have to jealously guard technology that has military applications. Let us realize that when we talk about "East-West technology transfer," we are not talking about a transfer of national assets in one direction—from West to East.

Defense Strategy

It is a primary mission of the Department to be prepared to wage war, because we invite aggression if we are unprepared to meet it, and we invite disaster if we are forced to meet aggression unprepared. The grim paradox we face, constantly, is that in trying to preserve peace with freedom we must strengthen ourselves with weapons we will never use if we are successful. We know from nearly 20 years' experience with the Soviets that unilateral restraint is the most dangerous of all policies and the policy most likely to produce expansionism or subjugation.

To fulfill our mission, we must restore our ability to mobilize our forces quickly and to support them in the combat we hope thus to deter. Accordingly, we have added major investments in readiness in our revisions of the fiscal year (FY) 1981–82 defense budgets.

But all the investments in equipment and personnel would not suffice if we are unprepared to respond adequately to warnings. And we have learned from history that warning of attack is often ambiguous. We must develop and implement improvements to strengthen our ability to respond to warning. We are acquiring better command and communications systems that are survivable and, thus, can properly function in a war.

The new Soviet projection forces do not merely give an unprecedented reach to Soviet military ventures into regions of greatest importance to us, but they are also inherently capable of swift execution. Hence, we have to be able to move our forces quickly. The scale and the speed of the invasion of Afghanistan has demonstrated that a country's capital and all its airfields can fall under Soviet military control in a matter of hours.

We must, frankly, recognize the possibility of a similar military operation against other countries where the Western interest would be vital. In the middle of any night, I may be awakened to be told that the Soviet Union is actually in the process of invading a country that we must defend but where we have neither bases nor troops. To be sure, we have contingency plans, but are our forces truly ready to carry them out? To be sure, there are crisis-management arrangements, but are we also administratively and psychologically ready to follow up with all the detailed steps necessary for farreaching and swift military movements? This is why I put so much stress on improving our ability to mobilize our forces and to mobilize quickly. We may not again have the preparation time we had to get ready for World War II, which was barely enough then.

Even more important, we have to build up a stronger military presence in vital areas to meet potential aggression before it can become an accomplished fact. This is the reason for the effort we now put into rapid deployment forces for the Middle East. This is also the reason for important elements in our security assistance bill, now pending before Congress, which is designed to help such countries as Turkey, Egypt, Sudan, and Israel.

However, within the next few years, we and our allies cannot rebuild our strength sufficiently to meet all risks of military aggression. Soviet-backed aggression against some of our vital interests in distant regions of the world might overwhelm some of our forces. What counts in a war is not winning the first battle, but the last. More and more it is apparent that we cannot and, indeed, should not rely exclusively on strategic forces and that we will need a strong conventional capacity to counter conventional strength that may be deployed against us.

We have to be prepared to launch counteroffensives in other regions and to exploit the aggressor's weaknesses wherever we might find them. That is to say, we must be prepared for waging a conventional war that may extend to many parts of the globe, if persistent local aggression by superior forces cannot be turned around. It is in this context that our need for naval superiority acquires special dimension.

Historically, we have always relied heavily on our industrial base. We recall how our productive genius was decisive in bringing us victory in both the great wars of this century. Today, we must, of course, rely on our ready nuclear forces to deter nuclear attack, as well as to help deter conventional attack against our principal alliance system. But our large and latent capacity to expand defense production has always provided an added and powerful deterrent against piecemeal aggression in other regions where we have vital interests.

Yet, we cannot take this asset for granted. Over the years, we have neglected our capacity to mobilize industry for defense. I have instituted changes in our methods for purchasing arms—the so-called acquisition process—designed to reduce costs and delays in our arms purchases in peacetime. In addition, these reforms will also improve our capability to mobilize industry in time of war or during a major emergency.

First, putting ourselves in a position to expand our defense effort greatly, if we should have to, will be a very low-cost aspect of our defense program, yet one that brings great returns in defending our security.

Second, such steps have particular importance in countries like ours. Democracies find it difficult to conduct and persevere in an active, long-term defense and foreign policy. As De Tocqueville long ago pointed out: "Foreign policies demand scarcely any of those qualities which are peculiar to democracy; they require, on the contrary, the perfect use of almost all those in which it is deficient." By the same token, democracies are naturally adverse to maintaining huge armaments and large bodies of men on a war footing in peacetime. We cannot hope, nor would we want to match our adversaries in ground forces during peace. Hence, the readiness with which we could mobilize our industrial potential serves as our countervailing reserve of military strength.

Now, as our defense policies are developed and put into

effect, some will carry on the earnest hunt for some easy label, some simplified tag to describe it so it will fit into a headline. I don't doubt that we will learn about "X's strategy," or "Y's doctrine." But in our fluid and complex world, the policies and doctrines that must guide our defense can never be final and complete, or be locked into dogmatic terms.

What we propose to do is clear. Why we do it should also be clear. There has been an enormous increase in Soviet strength. This is an ever-growing imbalance between their forces and ours.

We feel we must strengthen the deterrent capabilities of our nuclear forces and move to redress the present strategic imbalance.

We must maintain fully our conventional and nuclear deterrent commitment to NATO.

Our global interest and commitments dictate that our armed forces acquire greater range, mobility, and survivability. That means naval power able to command the sealanes vital to us and our allies. It means developing, urgently, a better ability to respond to crises far from our shores and to stay there as long as necessary.

The Arabian Gulf is such a vital area for us and our allies. The West's dependence on its oil means we must make sure we can respond effectively to threats in this region.

This idea that all conventional wars will be short has been overtaken by events. Conventional wars could come in all sizes; if we value our freedom, we must be able to defend ourselves in wars of any size and shape and in any region where we have vital interests.

We do not expect to do all these things overnight. Some of the tasks that face us are obviously continuing tasks. If we persevere—and the American people are determined to persevere—we can bring about changes not only in the strategic balance. Improved defense will bring with it greater international stability and a continuing hope that we can pass on to our descendants the inestimable privilege of peace with freedom.

LIMITS OF MILITARY POWER FOR
NATIONAL SECURITY[4]

After 35 years of a nuclear-military arms race, it is possible to define significant limits of military power for national security. Military superiority is undefinable and unattainable for each superpower. These same limits of military power also define new requirements for reversing the arms race.

In October, 1980, 60% of the U.S. public declared itself as favoring "U.S. seeking military superiority over the Soviet Union, not parity." Plainly, 60% of the U.S. population denies the reality of nuclear weapons and holds tenaciously to the mythology that it is still possible to be number one militarily and to use military power to dictate political terms in the fashion of the "unconditional surrender" model of World War II.

Underlying the long discussion of disarmament among nations has been the understanding that lowered levels of armaments produce mutual advantage: the prospect of physical destruction is reduced and the cost of armaments can be applied to constructive uses. Thus, the arms race from 1946 to 1981 between the U.S. and the Soviet Union has not improved the military security of either nation. . . . [The economic cost to the U.S. alone has exceeded $2,001,000,000,000.]

In 1961, I calculated that a rapid process of economic development for the unindustrialized people of the world could be executed with an annual capital outlay of about $22,000,-000,000. Hence, the arms race outlays by the U.S. and the Soviet Union during the last quarter-century would have financed 75 years of world economic development, while still leaving one-fourth of the actual budgets to be used for military security purposes.

[4] Excerpt from a magazine article "Limits of Military Power for National Security," by Seymour Melman, professor of industrial engineering, Columbia University. *USA Today.* 110:19–21. Jl. '81. Reprinted from *USA Today,* July 1981. Copyright © 1981 by the Society for the Advancement of Education.

Classically, attempts to negotiate international reduction and limitation on armaments levels were facilitated, as it was technically feasible to define armaments quantitatively and qualitatively. Owing to the evolution of military technology, these previously assumed conditions have altered. What is the unit weapon? One medium-sized military aircraft takes on altered military meaning when its weapons change from conventional to nuclear explosives. A missile with a conventional warhead is transformed by replacement with a nuclear warhead, or by 15 separately directed nuclear warheads.

Similar conditions have affected the qualitative assessment of weapons. A battleship was once more powerful than a destroyer. However, a motor torpedo boat, equipped to launch a nuclear-tipped missile, can destroy not only a single large naval vessel, but—conceivably—even an entire flotilla.

What is a "strategic" weapon? Is it to be measured by the explosive power of a warhead? If five "tactical" warheads are jointly applied, do they then become "strategic"? Does strategic mean the speed of delivery or the distance over which nonstop delivery can be affected? Is it reasonable to assume that great destructive force can be delivered only over great distances and at high speed? I pose these questions not only to suggest the new problem of defining terms of military "equality" or "parity" under conditions of nuclear weapons abundance, but, more importantly, because these questions reflect a true transformation in military power.

New Constraints on Military Power

Since the end of World War II, there have been many armed conflicts between the military forces of national states. However, it is a unique feature of this long period that in no case was such a conflict permitted to operate to a military conclusion. In each instance, other nations intervened, singly or through concerted action—as through the United Nations—to bring military operations to a halt well before one national power was able to overwhelm the other side militarily and then dictate political terms. The many lives lost in the procession of smaller wars from 1946 to 1971 rules out the possibility that a new concern for human life was the operating factor. Rather, this new development was a result of the well-founded and pervasive fear of the consequences from extension and escalation of what began, in each case, as limited national conflict. Extension means involving other countries; escalation means greater intensity of violence. The feared end result of military extension and escalation has been confrontation between superpowers resulting in nuclear war. That outcome cannot be excluded, since the generals of each superpower are trained to win and the weapons that each state wields in abundance will surely be brought to bear as one side or the other is at military disadvantage.

Today, the U.S. possesses 9,500 nuclear warheads fitted to long-range vehicles that could reach the U.S.S.R., while the Soviets wield about 7,000 warheads that could strike at the continental U.S. Smaller, "tactical" nuclear warheads are available in the tens of thousands.

In the U.S., there are 156 populated places with more than 100,000 persons each; in the U.S.S.R., there are about 220 such places.

By this reckoning, the American and the Soviet governments can each overkill the other's population-industrial centers more than 40 times over. This overkill development is absurd on both military and scientific grounds. What military advantage can possibly inhere in the ability to destroy more than once? What science suggests such a possibility?

The very military-technical pointlessness of the nuclear overkill buildup informs us to look elsewhere for an explanation of this bizarre development. Who gains? Within each state, the rulers gain in power over the industrial/scientific population that is harnessed for producing overkill and in power over the rest of each society that is trained to stand in awe of the leaders who are able to destroy us all.

With nuclear weapons available in large quantity, an overwhelming advantage was given to the offensive in military operations, for nuclear warheads of varied size—all immensely destructive—can be delivered by diverse means.

Against nuclear assault, there is no physical shield that can not be penetrated. Hence, the defense function is made unfeasible. In the presence of multiple overkill capability, allowances for weapons reliability do not alter the new military condition.

These characteristics of nuclear weapons affect the potential relationship between large and small military powers. As the knowledge for making nuclear weapons is elaborated and alternative technologies become available at lowered costs, it is not inconceivable that smaller nations will undertake the manufacture of their own nuclear weapons. However "small" such weapons and their numbers, the nature of nuclear weapons and the possibility of delivering them by alternative means opens up the nightmarish possibilities of military-political confrontations in which major powers find themselves confronted by small nations wielding nuclear "equalizers." What science or body of human wisdom could be drawn upon to advise a government on how much value to place on one of its cities?

The blast, fire, and radiation damage from major nuclear attacks would immediately destroy more than half of the U.S. and Soviet populations. In 1975, Dr. Philip Handler, president of the National Academy of Sciences, warned that, in a major nuclear war, the Earth's ozone layer would be damaged and that this "would persist for years, resulting in such intense ultra-violet irradiation of the Earth's surface as to cause crop failure by direct damage to plants and by major alterations of climate, and to induce intense sunburn in a few minutes and markedly increase the incidence of skin cancer in those exposed." We must thus infer that, even if either superpower could wipe out the opponent's nuclear forces by a flawless first strike, such success would alter the Earth's envelope, making the planet equally unlivable for the population of the "successful" attacker as for the rest of the human race.

Despite President Carter's Directive 59 on "limited" nuclear war, in a confrontation between nuclear-equipped armies, the side threatened with loss (while commanded to win) will bring up more-powerful conventional and nuclear weapons; then rapid nuclear escalation will occur with loss for all. (The "conventional-nuclear" strategy of the U.S. Army is set forth in U.S. Army Field Manual 100-5, *Operations*, 1976.)

Conventional Forces

In the relations of the nuclear superpowers, the consequences from use of conventional forces are not separable from nuclear forces, for each state trains and operates armed forces to apply successive intensities of force, as required to achieve military superiority. Recourse to nuclear weapons must therefore be expected.

Another major limit on modern military power concerns conventional warfare in its guerrilla form. Guerrilla warfare involves a major military-technical innovation. The innovation is of an organizational sort and does not consist primarily of particular weapons.

Guerrilla warfare involves military operations under the following conditions: a group sufficiently committed to a common purpose to risk their lives for achieving it; support from the surrounding population for the guerrilla fighting group; and inability of the opponent to differentiate the guerrillas from the surrounding population.

When these conditions are fulfilled, it has been unfeasible for large, well-equipped opposing armies to overcome the group so operating. This was starkly revealed in the frustration of the German army during World War II against the Yugoslav guerrillas, and is further demonstrated by the frustration of American armed forces in their relation to the guerrilla organization of the National Liberation Front in Vietnam and by the Soviet experience in Afghanistan.

There is no question that, in every department of weapons technology, American armed forces in Vietnam, and those supported by them, enjoyed overwhelming superiority. Still, the guerrilla opponent in Vietnam demonstrated military staying power despite the lack of heavy weapons, navy, or air force. The inability of the most elaborately equipped armed force in the world, backed by the world's largest military technology research and development network, to overcome the guerrilla forces of a small, poor country defines a major limit in military technology.

This is not to say that guerrilla operations can not be overcome. They can, if one or more of the three conditions listed above are altered. Thus, the second requirement: if the surrounding population is destroyed, then there is no "sea" in which the guerrillas can "swim." The U.S. has the capability for destroying populations in areas under guerrilla control, but such methods, until now, are unacceptable politically. Also, the destruction of a population goes counter to at least one traditional requirement of military operations: that the winner take control, not only of territory, but of the population therein.

The governments of the superpowers have each underwritten massive efforts to achieve superior military power. The advice they have followed in this respect has been based on assumptions which deserve review.

It has been assumed that military supremacy is both definable and achievable. In the case of nuclear warfare, this is clearly not the case. Neither is there any prospect, based on knowledge of nature or its application to technology, for supposing that this may be the case in some predictable future.

Once nuclear weaponry is understood as not being usable for military superiority, it is also difficult to suppose that conventional warfare, in the presence of nuclear options, can be turned to account for this purpose. If conventional weapons and forces are interlinked with nuclear weapons and forces, and the same men command the two and are indoctrinated to prevail, then it is plausible to expect that these men will move—given the need—from conventional to nuclear forces.

Perhaps the key technical assumption underlying confidence in the achievement of military superiority is the idea of "suboptimization," the strategy for improving a system as a whole through improvement of the parts. In military-technical form, this has meant an improved rifle, improved bullets, an improved airplane, an improved tire, an improved bandage, an improved uniform, an improved guidance system, an improved missile fuel—each one being pursued on the assumption that, from the sum of such unit technical improvements, there will emerge, necessarily, an improvement in a military system as a whole. . . .

Checkmating Conventional Strategy

This conventional strategy of military-technological development is checkmated by the two limits of military power discussed here—nuclear overkill and guerrilla warfare. "Improvement" in overkill is nonoperational and hence militarily, humanly, and scientifically meaningless. Ever-greater firepower for destroying an opponent under conditions of guerrilla warfare is meaningless, as the opponent can not be identified.

In weapons development, technological improvement has typically taken the form of attempts at superiority in destructive power, accuracy, speed, range, and reliability . . . Each of these developments might very well produce some particular military gain under conditions of World War II military operations. Once nuclear weapons are introduced in quantity, the military worth of these gains is vitiated.

This military-technical shopping list has its counterpart in agendas of particular technical problems being tackled by the military research and development institutions of the U.S. and the Soviet Union. Taken together, the interest in these developments rests on the assumption that military operations in some foreseeable future will be like the knightly joust of medieval warriors; wars that are fought between opposing armed forces such that the relative technological superiority of one as against the other might make some significant difference. Under present conditions, that prospect is unrealistic. In the era of nuclear overkill, knightly jousting between elite military forces is replaced by the prospect of nuclear confrontation and destruction of the human community.

A third assumption that is characteristically made with respect to military power is that, with enough money, superiority can be bought, but the limits defined here are independent of resource allocation. It is worth recalling the possibility that small countries may, in the near future, acquire nuclear weapons at relatively low cost.

What military operations can be performed without risking a loss while winning? A superpower can overwhelm a small country (the U.S., in the Dominican Republic in 1965; the Soviet Union, in Czechoslovakia in 1968), except where guerrilla forces resist (Vietnam, Afghanistan). Also, smaller countries can assault and exhaust each other if permitted by their weapons suppliers, the superpowers, as the Iraqi-Iranian war illustrates.

In sum, military technology can deliver great destructive power for operating a threat system; but military technology can not, now or in a foreseeable future, deliver either a military-political victory or a physical shield, that is defense, in nuclear war. Neither can present or foreseeable military technology insure victory against determined guerrilla opponents.

An important feature of the arms race has been the development of major military-industrial and military-technical institutions in major countries of the world. The long operation of such institutions and their large cadres of educated men gives institutional weight to the ideologies of the arms race, even when military programs are predictably checkmated by limits of military power.

Insofar as military technologists, however talented they may be individually, participate in what is scientifically absurd—like the multiplication of overkill, or the improvement of targeting accuracy of hundreds of yards in nuclear warheads with miles of destructive effect—then their technical work is in the tradition of science fiction, rather than science, regardless of its technical intricacy or elegance in detail.

The rulers of modern states and their military technologists promise, demagogically, to deliver something which, on the evidence, can no longer be achieved—military superiority in both nuclear and conventional warfare. When research organizations, for example, reach limits of the potential contribution to given technology, as in the case of most military research institutions, how can one account for the perpetuation of such organizations? The answer must be sought in the realm of social laws of perpetuation of organizations and the decision power of rulers: social inertia and power that stems from the well-esteemed operation of a large organization that has high status, large budgets, a technically qualified staff, and a network of interrelations with important institutions in society. Thus, military research establishments sustain operations through the promise of military-technological "improvement," always implying that their cumulative result will be the devoutly desired superiority—that is now checkmated by the limits of military power.

Correction of all recently noted American military "deficiencies" offers no escape from the limits of military power. No improvements in number, size, accuracy, reliability, or speed of weapons and forces can break through the overkill limit.

Furthermore, error and failure are unavoidable both in people and mechanisms, as repeated nuclear false alarms have illustrated. As powerful weapons are multiplied, no safeguards can preclude catastrophic accidents.

Denial of military reality serves various interests. For government managers, the armed forces and a military economy have been mainstays for empire-building at home and *Pax Americana* abroad; for corporate managers, a military economy assures risk-free profit. While the business press assails American managers for failing the nation by fostering industrial incompetence, appeals to nationalist nostalgia and primitive "we'll show 'em" militarism are welcome diversions. Many are receptive to hypernationalism because fundamentalist religiosity is often permeated with worship of the nation-state, a form of idolatry There is, however, unattended by establishment consensus, a military agreement. In 1962, the superpowers separately detailed plans for agreed, inspected reversal of the arms race. The proposals were never negotiated. Our government does not employ a single person with responsibility for thinking about reversing the arms race. The establishment's refusal even to try for this alternative may go down as the crime of the century—if there is anyone around to know it.

II. NUCLEAR ARMS AND ARMS CONTROL

EDITOR'S INTRODUCTION

Nuclear weapons are the most serious problem facing each President of the United States. For the past twenty years, the United States and the Soviet Union have attempted to limit their nuclear arsenals by mutual agreement. Presidents Carter and Leonid Brezhnev signed the Strategic Arms Limitation Treaty (SALT II) at their Vienna summit meeting in June 1979. But President Carter removed the treaty from Senate consideration after the Soviet invasion of Afghanistan in December 1979. In 1981, President Reagan and the Republican majority in the Senate had no intention of ratifying this treaty, which they regarded as "fatally flawed." Lacking a new accord, the administration said it would abide by the terms of SALT II as long as the Soviets did, but that it did not feel legally bound to uphold them.

Opening this section, Barry M. Blechman, writing in *Foreign Affairs*, explores the history of the strategic arms negotiations. He believes that these negotiations were based on public expectations, ultimately unfulfilled, of achieving arms reductions. Because the negotiations' results fell far short, the public judged the SALT process harshly. Nonetheless, the author believes that arms control can continue to make an important contribution to U.S. security.

The second article is an excerpt from a July 1981 speech by Secretary of State Alexander M. Haig. The speech was intended to convince the American public that the Reagan administration was serious about its commitment to arms control. Haig outlines a series of principles which, he believes, will restore tough-mindedness and realism to the U.S. side of the negotiating table.

Article three, a White House background text, outlines the Reagan administration's plans for modernizing the U.S. strategic bomber fleet and land-based missile forces. Articles

four and five, excerpted from the *New York Times*, examine
the merits of the President's program. The final article is an
excerpt from a November 1981 speech by President Reagan,
his most important arms control initiative to date. Reagan
proposed the "zero-option" for Europe: the United States will
cancel its plans to install new medium-range missiles in Europe if the Soviets agree to remove the SS–4s, SS–5s and
SS–20s which they have already installed in Europe.

DO NEGOTIATED ARMS LIMITATIONS
HAVE A FUTURE?[1]

As we enter the fall of 1980, the future of efforts to limit
armaments through international negotiations is very much in
doubt. President Carter's decision in January to defer Senate
debate on the SALT II treaty only recognized formally what
had long been apparent: in many ways the troubled history of
SALT II already had represented a significant, perhaps fatal,
defeat for negotiated arms limitations—regardless of the specific fate of the treaty itself. Even before the Soviet occupation of Afghanistan, enthusiasm for arms limitations had become increasingly restrained within the administration (to
put it mildly) as the SALT agreement's political problems had
become increasingly evident. Moreover, the national SALT
debate and related developments had occasioned perceptions
in the Congress and among the public at large of political and
substantive liabilities of negotiated arms limitations that
seemed likely to give pause to any President in 1981.

Few would have predicted such a state of affairs. Upon
taking office, President Carter set ambitious objectives for,
and assigned unprecedented priority to, arms limitations. The
design of the MX missile system, for example, the most ex-

[1] Reprint of an article "Do Negotiated Arms Limitations Have a Future?" by
Barry M. Blechman, Senior Associate at the Carnegie Endowment for International
Peace. *Foreign Affairs*. 59:102–25. Fall '80. Reprinted by permission of Foreign Affairs.
Copyright © 1980 by the Council on Foreign Relations, Inc.

pensive weapons program backed by the Carter administration, was strongly influenced by projected requirements for verifying future negotiated limitations on strategic weapons. Similarly, early in 1977 the President established tough unilateral policies aimed at reducing the risk of nuclear proliferation and restraining sales of conventional weapons. Most important, in March 1977, U.S. objectives in the ongoing SALT negotiations were reevaluated and a more ambitious negotiating position adopted. At the same time, then, Secretary of State Cyrus Vance proposed the creation of new U.S.-Soviet arms limitation working groups. Eight such groups were agreed upon: antisatellite weapons, chemical weapons, civil defense, comprehensive nuclear test ban, conventional arms transfers, demilitarization of the Indian Ocean, prior notification of missile tests, and radiological weapons and new types of mass destruction weapons.

The results of this ambitious program have been modest. Indeed, in the closing months of the present administration, efforts to place limitations on armaments have been at a standstill, their prognosis bleak.

Judged strictly on their own criteria, unilateral efforts to reduce the risk of nuclear proliferation and to restrain arms sales may have made progress for a time, but seem to have accomplished little of permanence. During the second half of 1979, as concern about the substantive and political consequences of Soviet military assertiveness mounted within the administration, the President reversed himself on a series of arms transfer decisions, authorizing sales of ov-10 aircraft to Morocco and of large quantities of munitions to Saudi Arabia, and making a crucial blanket exception to the arms transfer restraint policy by permitting development of a new aircraft whose only markets would be found overseas. Similarly, efforts to restrain nuclear proliferation were set back in 1979 by the ambiguous results of the International Nuclear Fuel Cycle Evaluation (INFCE) study, several international deals involving components of civilian nuclear power systems, an unexplained event near South Africa which could have been a nuclear explosion, and the administration's reversal of prior decisions not to provide economic or military assistance to Pakistan because of that nation's program to develop a nuclear explosive capability. While these individual decisions may be understandable in the light of world events, and although the nonproliferation and arms transfer policies did score some important early successes, at the end of three years both policies clearly were taking second place to more traditional concerns.

Even greater disappointments occurred in the negotiations. The SALT II negotiations were concluded successfully, but the treaty's fate is at best uncertain. Of the U.S.-Soviet working groups, negotiations on civil defense and prior notification of missile tests were never held; three negotiations which did begin have since been terminated—in fact, if not formally; and two negotiations—for a comprehensive nuclear test ban and a ban on chemical weapons—continue, but with no agreement in sight. Agreement also remains elusive in a negotiation already proceeding when President Carter took office: talks for mutual and balanced force reductions in Europe. Only one negotiation was concluded successfully: that on radiological weapons; elements of an agreement acceptable to both the United States and the Soviet Union have been presented to the U.N. Committee on Disarmament for consideration and possible inclusion in a multilateral treaty.

Why was it not possible to accomplish more? To be sure, these activities were pursued in a domestic environment that included the same social and political factors which in recent years have made virtually any national policy difficult to establish and even harder to sustain over the long term. The absence of a national consensus, the dispersion of power within the Congress, the continuing conflict between the executive and legislative branches over appropriate roles in foreign policy decision-making, the legacy of suspicion and distrust of the presidency inherited by Jimmy Carter, the erosion of the major political parties and the rise of single-issue interest groups—all contributed to the difficulties of U.S. foreign policy in general and U.S. arms limitation efforts in particular.

Moreover, the climate for arms limitations had been

strongly and adversely affected by the continuing buildup of Soviet military power. Roughly 16 years in duration by 1980, the broad scope and relentless pace of the buildup has had dramatic effects on western public and elite perceptions of the political and military implications of U.S.-Soviet arms negotiations. Although these Soviet military efforts raise certain specific security concerns, their perhaps more important effects are diffuse and political in character. The Soviet Union's continued willingness to allocate a relatively large percentage of its relatively scarce resources to military forces which already—to a western eye—appear excessive for defensive purposes, has raised the most serious questions about Soviet ambitions.

Continuing turbulence and frequent military conflicts in the third world have seriously aggravated the situation. These conflicts, which more often than not have challenged a status quo favoring the West, pose problems enough. Direct or indirect Soviet involvement, when it occurs, adds another and more threatening dimension to third world turmoil. To be sure, these Soviet military programs and activity in the third world do not violate any arms control agreement. Moreover, short of war, negotiating mutual limitations on armaments remains the only direct way to constrain Soviet armed forces. Yet the political logic of the situation even before the occupation of Afghanistan was such that Soviet military decisions clearly made efforts to form and sustain the constituencies necessary to ensure the success of arms limitations initiatives far more difficult.

The U.S. Senate's SALT deliberations are instructive. At the end of the first round of the Senate Foreign Relations Committee hearings in August 1979, prospects for the treaty seemed bright. Criticisms of the specific terms of the treaty aired during the extensive sessions of the committee had been fully discussed and largely discredited. Remaining concerns focused mainly on what commitments to military spending the Carter administration would be willing to make to offset charges that SALT could induce a certain euphoria in the U.S. government and among the public which would lead to neglect of the defense budget. Although passage was far from certain, betting in Washington was that approval by the full Senate would be in hand by Thanksgiving. The subsequent travails of the treaty are traceable not to the surfacing of any new arguments about the agreement itself, nor to new information about the balance of strategic weapons, but to other types of events. The revelation in September that there was a Soviet combat brigade in Cuba and the subsequent pseudo-crisis delayed the committee markup. Once sufficient time had passed for the hoopla to die down, the committee reviewed the treaty line by line, again demonstrating the weaknesses of substantive criticisms of the agreement itself. The treaty was passed by the full committee in November without amendments significant enough to require renegotiation. Then, however, came the seizure of the U.S. Embassy in Tehran, which delayed the opening of floor debate, and, finally, the *coup de grace* administered by the Soviet occupation of Afghanistan.

What now? Obviously, not much will happen in the near term—at least through the U.S. election. But what of the period after 1980? Should there be continued efforts to limit arms through negotiations? What objectives, if any, are realistic? Much will depend upon the resolution of two fundamental issues: the continuing debate about the desired character of U.S.-Soviet relations, and a largely unstated argument about the role of nuclear weapons in U.S. foreign policy.

II

Surveying the connection between U.S.-Soviet relations and the progress of arms negotiation over the past ten years, it is worth recalling the words of Vladimir S. Semyonov, who began the Soviet presentation at the first session of the Strategic Arms Limitation Talks in 1969:

The government of the U.S.S.R. attaches great importance to the negotiations on curbing the strategic arms race. Their positive results should undoubtedly contribute both to improvement in Soviet-American relations and in the consolidation of universal peace.

Thus, at the very outset of the talks, the concept which eventually was to break the back of the SALT process was recognized formally: linkage, the idea that progress toward arms limitation would lead to progress in other aspects of U.S.-Soviet relations, and, conversely, its corollary, that cooperation (or lack of cooperation) in other aspects of U.S.-Soviet relations would facilitate (or hamper) movement in arms negotiations. Both the United States and the Soviet Union have been ambivalent about "linkage." Each has stressed or deemphasized "linkage" when it was in its own interest to do so. In the end, however, the concept took firm root in the American political system and, as a result, imposed a heavier burden on the talks than they could possibly bear; indeed, the notion implied a model of U.S.-Soviet relations which was strongly opposed by a variety of groups with powerful voices in national security decision-making.

Given their ideological origins, it would be surprising if Soviet commentators did not stress interrelationships between negotiated arms limitations and broader accommodation between the United States and the Soviet Union. From a Marxist theoretical perspective, the source of all conflict is economic and by extension political, stemming fundamentally from the existence of historically antagonistic social systems. To a Marxist theorist, the basic premise of arms control—that weapons in themselves contribute to the risk of war—is sophistry. Conflict results from the necessary clash of opposing social forces. The alleviation of conflict, therefore, can only result from broad political accommodation. By making preexisting settlements specific and legally binding, arms limitation agreements can strengthen political accommodations but they can never force new arrangements; they are the "practical embodiment" of détente, not its cause.

At times, the Soviets have been willing to demonstrate the practical consequences of this relationship. Perhaps the best example occurred in December 1978. At that time, Secretary

Vance met with Soviet Foreign Minister Andrei Gromyko in Geneva in what was widely viewed as likely to be the final round of substantive SALT II negotiations. Indeed, the White House had begun media preparations to announce completion of the agreement. Just prior to the round, however, the United States declared its intention to normalize relations with China, a process to be marked by the visit of Deputy Premier Deng Xiaoping to Washington the following month. In response, the Soviets demonstrated their belief that political conditions were not yet right for U.S.-Soviet arms limitations by elevating to new prominence at the final session what previously had been perceived as relatively minor issues, thus delaying the U.S.-Soviet summit expected to cap the negotiations.

For the most part, however, the close linkage between movement in broader political relations and progress in arms limitations which would seem to be dictated by Soviet theory has not proved to be important in practice. Most notably, in 1972 the Soviets completed SALT I as scheduled, despite the United States' mining of Haiphong and other North Vietnamese ports on the eve of the summit (an act which trapped or damaged a number of Soviet-flag merchant ships). More recently, the Soviets have vigorously protested U.S. attempts to link progress in arms negotiation to the curtailment of Soviet military activities in Africa, Cuba and South Asia.

To be sure, Soviet forebearance did not result either from devotion to the cause of arms limitation or from a rejection of their Marxist heritage in favor of historic American pragmatism. What did happen was that the stream of world events and the dictates of Soviet internal politics were such that the Brezhnev regime found pursuit of SALT very much in its interest, despite continued erosion of the broader context of U.S.-Soviet relations. In fact, as U.S.-Soviet relations deteriorated, the Soviets pressed harder across the range of negotiations, adopting increasingly conciliatory positions and raising expectations in several. It is as if they saw in arms limitation negotiations the only remaining evidence of the possibility of U.S.-Soviet cooperation, and clung to them in desperation as Brezhnev's policy of détente otherwise was torn asunder.

In the United States, the experience has been just the opposite. The American theory of arms control would isolate such negotiations from politics. In theoretical terms, arms limitation talks should be viewed as technical exercises, directed at constraining the risks which weapons themselves add to existing political conflicts. As those espousing arms control made no pretense of solving political conflicts through the negotiations they proposed, they saw no relationship (other than that artificially instilled by politicians) between progress or lack of progress in settling underlying sources of conflict and progress or lack of progress in arms negotiations. Indeed, they accepted international tensions as inevitable and saw arms limitation talks simply as one way to manage their more dangerous consequences.

In practice, however, the United States has closely linked movement in arms control with broader political accommodation with the Soviet Union. Specifically, successive U.S. administrations, perhaps reluctantly, have frequently concluded that there could not be movement in arms talks unless or until the Soviet Union modified its international behavior so as not to pose military challenges to Western interests. Examples are legion. The start of the talks, for example, planned for 1968, was delayed by the occupation of Czechoslovakia. In 1976, completion of the Vladivostok accord was deferred because of Soviet military involvement in Angola. And, despite its public protestations to the contrary, as early as 1978 the Carter administration's positions in SALT and other arms negotiations were strongly influenced by the deterioration of U.S.-Soviet relations, punctuated by such events as the Soviet military involvement in the Horn of Africa and the East German and Cuban roles in the Shaba incident in Zaïre.

This sensitivity on the part of American policymakers should be expected in a democratic political system. Policies—especially innovative policies that run counter to traditional ways of doing business—cannot be sustained without substantial political constituencies. SALT suffered more from rising uneasiness among the American populace about Soviet military power and Soviet assertiveness than from any deficiencies of its own. Never mind that SALT was the one policy instrument that conceivably could place limits on Soviet forces. The concept that prevailed in the public's mind extended the basic premise of linkage (i.e., that progress in arms control could facilitate progress in broader relations) to an assertion that if arms control was worth pursuing, it would result in broader accommodation. Since there was no evidence of such a broad accommodation, the argument ran, then obviously arms control was at least not serving its purposes and probably, in some mysterious way, was itself contributing to the problem. As this concept took root, first among conservative Republicans and later in a broader segment of the public, both the Ford and Carter administrations felt compelled to behave as though they accepted it as well.

In effect, the SALT talks became a weathervane of U.S.-Soviet relations, the centerpiece and primary symbol of a certain model of that relationship. As such, the talks were criticized by, indeed contributed to, the creation of a coalition of dedicated opponents who fought both the treaties and the process which led to them, as much for what they implied for U.S.-Soviet relations as for whatever specific limitations they did or did not impose on American and Soviet nuclear weapons.

The 1972 treaty which placed severe limitations on anti-ballistic missile (ABM) systems is the key factor here. By agreeing not to deploy weapons that could create the illusion of a capability to defend against a major nuclear attack, the two nations formally recognized the probability that each would suffer unprecedented destruction in the event of a major nuclear exchange. Thus, they accepted the necessity for a certain degree of cooperation in their relations and implicitly set limits on their competition. This is not to say that they agreed to get along with one another, to end the rivalry, or anything like that; far from it. Still, they did establish a formally recognized mutual need to stop the competition from getting out of hand, to avoid confrontations that could contain a real danger of nuclear war.

The ABM treaty is thus a central element in the quest for cooperative U.S.-Soviet relations. The continuing SALT process supported the viability of the ABM treaty; limits on defensive weapons probably cannot be sustained in the presence of a wide-open offensive weapons race. SALT thus came to symbolize America's acceptance of the need to get along with the Soviet Union. Additionally, by linking the United States and the U.S.S.R. in a cooperative venture reserved for them and no other nations, SALT set the two superpowers apart from all other states—even America's allies.

To many Americans these postures are wrong, both morally and in terms of U.S. security interests. They believe that the United States must seek to change Soviet society and, that to do so, it must remain in a state of tension with the Soviet government. They argue that if it is isolated, the Soviet state eventually will crack of its own internal contradictions—nationalities problems, economic failures, corruption, the natural yearnings of individuals for freedom, and so forth. This means that the United States should seek to construct a wall of implacable hostility around the U.S.S.R., a political-cum-military alliance among the nations of Western Europe, Japan, China and others in the Third World. Only America can galvanize such an alliance, it is argued, and to do so the United States must avoid bilateral agreements or even bilateral negotiations, as these imply permanent acceptance of the Soviet regime and accord legitimacy to it. The ABM treaty, the SALT II treaty, and the SALT process itself—to say nothing of other arms negotiations—are thus seen to undermine the long-run objective of causing fundamental change in Soviet society.

Obviously, opponents of arms limitations typically find it in their interest not to articulate this line of reasoning; they prefer to debate technical points in the treaty itself, arguing that they support arms control in the abstract, but that a better deal should have been made. The reasons for this stance are clear: the specter of unfettered and open-ended competition with the Soviet Union, including a relatively high risk of confrontation and nuclear war, is not one likely to find substantial political support over the long term. The fact that the congressional SALT debate concentrated on technical questions, rather than basic issues like the implications of the SALT process for U.S.-Soviet relations, testifies to the political skills of the treaty's opponents. The importance of their ability to dictate the terms of the debate is magnified when the second unstated burden of SALT is considered.

It is widely believed in the United States that nuclear weapons can play only a small and tightly circumscribed role in foreign policy. Because of the tremendous risks they imply, the standard argument proceeds, nuclear weapons (meaning nuclear threats) can be utilized only for narrow and quite specific purposes. First and foremost, they serve to deter nuclear attacks on, or coercion of, the United States itself. Additionally, it is believed, the U.S. nuclear umbrella can be extended to a few other nations—primarily the industrialized democracies. And that, more or less, is that. It is true that beginning in the early 1970s some officials began to speak of additional purposes for nuclear weapons, as when discussing limited nuclear options, but this was strictly in a reactive context, to offset the presumed political consequences of growth in Soviet nuclear capabilities.

Some argue, however, that the *threat* of nuclear war should be integrated more centrally into U.S. foreign policy; nuclear strength could be translated into political clout in a positive and assertive way. Indeed, some would maintain that this has already occurred, and continues to occur, regardless of our declaratory stance. Ever since World War II, they argue, nuclear weapons in fact have provided the one trump card in the U.S. hand. From the two bombs dropped on Japan, to nuclear threats, implicit or explicit, during the Berlin blockade, Korean War, Quemoy crisis, Cuban missile crisis, and 1973 Middle East war, as well as other more uncertain occasions, the United States turned to the threat of its nuclear arsenal, when push came to shove, to protect its own security and the security of its friends and allies.

Faced with the impossibility, in a democracy, of sustaining over the long haul conventional forces large enough to match those of the Soviet Union—this reasoning continues—the United States will likely confront this necessity again. NATO doctrine itself ensures such a probability with its explicit reliance on the threat of first use of nuclear weapons in the event that conventional conflict goes badly. Moreover, the balance of conventional military power is turning so adversely against the United States that this reliance is more and more likely. Witness the recent tentative turn to nuclear threats to back up President Carter's commitment that the United States would defend the Persian Gulf from Soviet aggression.

To the extent that the United States must rely on nuclear weapons, it is argued, agreements which seek to enshrine strategic nuclear parity as a permanent condition of U.S.-Soviet relations are misguided; rather, the United States must turn its resources and technology to the quest for strategic superiority. Not that success in this goal is seriously contemplated; none but the most naïve believe that such an end is attainable. Nonetheless, the argument runs, by placing itself formally in a posture of seeking nuclear superiority the United States would be demonstrating a willingness to manipulate the risk of nuclear war for political objectives, thus lending credibility to the nuclear threats implicit in its foreign policy. In short, only in an environment of wide-open U.S.-Soviet nuclear competition can the United States' *necessary reliance* on nuclear weapons to underpin its foreign policy be supported successfully.

An element uniting these two underlying strands of argumentation against SALT—implications for U.S.-Soviet relations and for the role of nuclear weapons in foreign policy—is that those adhering to these viewpoints cannot be satisfied by any changes in the specific content of agreements. From their perspectives, the adverse implications of SALT can be erased only when the very process of seeking arms limitation comes to an end, and its meager products are dismantled.

III

Obviously, those who oppose SALT for these reasons can never be counted among the potential supporters of future arms control initiatives. But what of others? Can a new coalition be created with sufficient political power to rejuvenate arms negotiations?

Rebuilding such a constituency would necessarily be complicated by the ambivalence which characterizes American attitudes toward the talks. Even among supporters, the purposes and potential benefits of arms negotiations have reflected sharply divergent perspectives. This is symbolized by the very title of the agency created in 1961 to plan and carry out these negotiations—the United States Arms Control and Disarmament Agency, a title which emerged only after long debate, in a typical congressional compromise that appeared to give each side what it wanted but in fact gave neither the benefits of victory. For "arms control" and "disarmament" represent quite different approaches to arms limitations, with very different policy implications. Although obfuscation of the differences between them did help to secure a prominent position for arms limitations on the nation's agenda for a while, in the end it contributed to the failure of efforts to negotiate limits on armaments.

The theory of "arms control" is based on the rather modest notion that decisions to acquire certain types or quantities of weapons can aggravate political conflicts and thereby *in themselves contribute to the risk of war*. This is not to say that weapons decisions are a primary or even secondary cause of conflict; only that such decisions are one factor which influences the relative probabilities that political conflicts are resolved peacefully, remain unsettled, or result in war. It is assumed that one nation's weapons decisions are perceived and interpreted by other states, and that these judgments influence the latters' assessments of the potential military threat to their security, the likelihood that their adversaries intend to make use of that potential, and what weapons or military actions in response are necessary on their own part. Thus the initial decision and the decisions which follow affect both the "stability" (a key word) of the military balance and of broader political relations among nations, as well as the risk of war. Conversely, the theory continues, these adverse effects can be reduced, or at least contained, both through unilateral decisions to avoid deployments of "destabilizing" weapons and, more important, through international negotiations on agreements to mutually avoid deploying certain types of weapons or to place other types of agreed mutual limitations on weaponry.

Thus, at its root, "arms control" offers a technically oriented approach to arms limitations with a modest set of objectives. It accepts conflict among nations as an inevitable part of contemporary international politics and views military force as a necessary (and legitimate) instrument of national policy. It views negotiated limitations on armaments solely as a means of containing the risks and costs of political conflict. "Arms control" and military programs are seen as two sides of the same coin, both being means of enhancing the nation's security.

The limited objectives of arms control flow from its recognition of the fundamental political basis of international conflict, and its acceptance that essentially technical discussions about weapons can only reflect, not initiate, political accommodation. In the usual formulation, three goals are mentioned: (a) to reduce the risk of war; (b) to reduce the cost of preparing for war; and (c) to reduce the cost of war should it occur. In all three, however, success can come only at the margin. The purpose is not to abolish war, but to diminish the risk that war would occur. The objective is not to turn all swords into plowshares, but to create conditions wherein some resources which otherwise might be used to prepare for war can instead be utilized for peaceful purposes.

As this modest theoretical construct (of interest chiefly to a handful of defense intellectuals and military specialists) was transformed into a national political issue, however, these objectives and even the ultimate promise of arms control were sharply revised. Essentially, the nation's political leaders found in arms control a convenient means of satisfying popular demands resulting both from international circumstances and certain fundamental strands of opinion long present in the nation's psyche. These latter—*inter alia,* anti-militarism, with its concomitant desire to minimize defense spending, and an aversion to power politics, especially a fear of foreign entanglements—had dominated the nation's foreign policies (except for a few short-lived periods) until the Second World War. They remain important determinants of certain basic American perspectives on world affairs, and can become more or less so depending on events. For convenience, I will refer to those whose attitudes on world affairs are dominated by these sorts of concerns as the "disarmament constituency." Readers should be clear, however, that this shorthand refers to a far larger group than that small minority which actively supports true disarmament.

In the late 1950s and early 1960s, concerns of the "disarmament constituency" concentrated largely on nuclear weapons. After all, at that time, the tensions of cold war confrontation in Berlin and elsewhere were very real. The dangers of nuclear holocaust, still at the forefront of concern for the postwar generation which dominated political life, were manifest through such phenomena as civil defense drills and atmospheric nuclear tests, to say nothing of the surviving victims of the Hiroshima and Nagasaki bombs. Ten years later, in the late 1960s, the concerns of the disarmament constituency were far broader, its demands more strident, and its political clout far more impressive. Twenty years later, in the late 1970s, as memories of Vietnam faded, as increasing Soviet assertiveness revitalized old fears of Russian imperialism, and as events in Africa and Southwest Asia demonstrated anew the potential utility of military power, attitudes which motivate the disarmament constituency have again been subsumed by other concerns.

For those 20 years, however, American political leaders found in arms control a pragmatic means of satisfying the demands of this constituency—at least for a while. Thus, for example, as his administration came increasingly under fire because of the slow pace of disengagement from Southeast Asia, President Nixon found it increasingly in his interest to emphasize SALT. In effect, the Nixon administration said, "Yes, we know you are dissatisfied with what is happening in Southeast Asia and we are doing our best, under difficult circumstances, to speed things up. But, anyway, look over here. We have managed to isolate Vietnam from U.S.-Soviet relations and are making important progress. We are building a 'structure of peace' with the Russians, a structure whose centerpiece is SALT—the control of nuclear weapons. This will be of lasting benefit for your concerns."

This is not to imply that the Nixon administration's SALT policies were cynically motivated or driven solely by a desire to ease the pressures stemming essentially from the war; simply that, because of the war, the separate effort to control nuclear weapons gained new political significance and therefore greater emphasis. Nor is it being suggested that only the Nixon administration acted from this complex of motives. At times Presidents Kennedy, Johnson, Ford and Carter all found political benefits in their support for arms control, and saw in their advocacy of arms control a means of satisfying political demands. Indeed, if anything, Democratic Presidents are more susceptible to the pressures of the disarmament constituency. For example, although his personal commitment to arms limitation is beyond question, President Carter obviously saw the benefit of a strong pro-arms control stance when competing for the support of the then-McGovern wing of the party during the early stages of his presidential campaign.

Regardless of who was President, however, these political ends necessitated the transformation of the limited objectives of arms control into *first steps*. The implicit promise was that the arms control process would continue, and that each stage would have more ambitious goals. In this way, the disarmament constituency could accept tentative and modest early measures; political support was exchanged for the promise of more ambitious undertakings in the future.

It is surprising that this deal survived as long as it did. The premises upon which it was based simply could not be fulfilled, and evidence to that effect soon became apparent. After all, the 1963 Limited Test Ban Treaty did not soon result in a comprehensive end to nuclear testing. Treaties in the 1960s to demilitarize the Antarctic, outer space, and the seabed were not soon followed by progress toward demilitarization of regions in which the threat of military conflict was more pertinent. And, most important, the SALT I Interim Agreement on Offensive Weapons did not quickly lead to more significant constraints on nuclear weapons as had been promised.

It took the SALT II Treaty, however, for the bargain finally to come unstuck. SALT II would place many important restraints on U.S. and Soviet nuclear weapons, restraints which could significantly stabilize the nuclear competition and the balance of strategic forces, thereby contributing to a lower risk of nuclear war. Its features in this regard—limits on the number of warheads on strategic missiles, limits on the introduction of new types of land-based missiles, a special sub-ceiling on the number of land-based missiles with multiple warheads, and others—were readily recognizable to the specialist in arms control. However, the importance of these things was not nearly so apparent to the general public, nor to most politicians. What the latter looked for were the obvious—the signs of progress toward disarmament, toward fulfillment of the promise attributed to arms control 20 years before. And these did not exist. The treaty would cause only slight reductions in Soviet nuclear forces, and, in fact, would ratify an increase in U.S. forces. The treaty would not end weapons modernization, and thereby permit budget reductions—far from it. It would allow an acceleration of U.S. strategic programs and thereby larger expenditures on strategic forces. For all these reasons, the treaty disappointed the disarmament constituency.

The effect of this was not so much to lose specific senatorial votes for ratification as to make it impossible to organize a political constituency behind the treaty. For the most part, the Carter administration's efforts to gain support for the treaty were ignored—not so much because of anything deleterious in the treaty itself, as because of its lack of evident positive attributes. Its importance was simply not credible (and certainly not obvious) to a significant political audience. As a result, mass support could not be enlisted and senators, for the most part, had little if any reason to get out in front of the ratification process. What could they cite in their home states as reason for their advocacy? That the treaty would result in "only" 2,250 central strategic nuclear delivery systems on each side? That, like SALT I, the new treaty was important not for itself, but because it would make possible future negotiations? After ten years of SALT, the promise of significant future gains would no longer wash.

Moreover, inflated expectations of the ultimate promise of negotiated arms limitations had the contradictory effect of stiffening the opposition. As the objectives of arms control were transformed from the modest goal of regulating the nuclear competition into "the elimination of all nuclear weapons from this earth," as President Carter put it in his inaugural address, the coalition of groups opposing SALT grew and hardened. Apart from the opposition already identified, others opposed SALT because its transfigured objectives directly challenged their personal and institutional interests. Obviously, individuals whose entire professional lives have been devoted to the development or operation of nuclear forces are likely to view these weapons in a rather more favorable light than was indicated by the administration's policy. Still others grew disenchanted as they saw a certain naïveté in the inflated rhetoric. While both these groups may support negotiations which seek to regulate the nuclear competition, they are unlikely to believe that a process that aims ultimately to abolish nuclear weapons is either realistic or beneficial.

As the post-Vietnam retrenchment in U.S. military power

continued through the 1970s, SALT increasingly lost the support it previously enjoyed from the armed services, from the aerospace industry and the labor unions which serve it, from the scientific and research community associated with the Defense Department, and from their political representatives. This was a crucial defeat for arms control; without the support of these groups and in the absence of prospective treaties dramatic enough to stimulate decisive political support from the disarmament constituency, arms limitations can never succeed in a democratic political system.

The regulation of international trade provides an analogy of some relevance. The strongest supporters of international trade agreements typically are those firms and labor organizations that are most dependent upon imports and exports for their livelihoods. Besides their obvious interest in liberalized trade policy, they see in regulation the benefits of stability, which permit effective long-range planning, as well as the avoidance of risks and costs of unfettered competition. Theoretically at least, those most directly concerned with the strategic competition could see similar benefits in arms control. Yet, since 1972, this has not proven to be the case, largely, in my view, because of exaggeration of the original goals of arms control and obfuscation of the differences between arms control and disarmament.

If efforts to negotiate limits on arms are to succeed in the future, policymakers will have to choose between two alternatives. They can define, structure and pursue these efforts along the lines of the original concept of arms control, seeking modest objectives, and enlisting the support of those elements of the government, industry, labor, and the scientific community which are most personally and directly concerned with nuclear weapons; or they can continue to blur the distinction between arms control and disarmament, seeking to reinvigorate that wider political constituency whose roots lie in considerations of religion, morality and the fundamental American antipathy to military power. The latter approach can succeed, however, only if the products of negotiations are more dramatic than those recently delivered. If this wider constituency is to be rebuilt, the benefits of agreements will have to be apparent, on their merits, to a large popular audience. As there is little basis in either the history of arms negotiations or in more recent developments in U.S.-Soviet relations to believe that such dramatic results are at all feasible, a return to the original concept of arms control is clearly warranted.

IV

Ironically, the failure of the Carter administration's arms control policy, and particularly the failure of SALT II in the 96th Congress, could provide an opportunity to modify and then revitalize the public's appreciation of arms control. This would not be easy; it would take considerable time. It would require the leadership of the administration that takes office in 1981 and the support of those in the Congress who have developed a reputation for expertise on the subject.

Essentially, these political leaders would have to make clear to the public that no matter what happens in arms negotiations, for the foreseeable future the United States will have to take decisive and costly actions to rebuild its military forces sufficiently to offset the growth in Soviet military power over the past 16 years. Given that such a defense build-up is vigorously pursued, however, the extent of the effort required and the dangers implicit in the continuing competition may be moderated through agreements placing mutual restraints on specific types of weapons. If other nations agree to place specific limits on the size of their forces, for example, the United States may be in a position to accept comparable restrictions on its own forces. If other nations agree to retard certain weapons modernization programs, the United States may be able to slow down some of its programs to a comparable degree. If other nations agree to restrict the operational flexibility of their forces in a certain region in order to avoid suspicions about the possible outbreak of war, then the United States may find that it too has an interest in limiting the flexibility of its forces in comparable ways.

In short, if arms control is to be revived, policymakers and political opinion leaders should be forthright about the modest potential of even successful negotiations. Arms talks can reduce the risk of war, but not abolish war. Arms talks can reduce the cost of preparing for war, but the burden of military preparations will remain high as long as the international political system remains in its present form. Agreements that result from arms negotiations are not stepping stones to peace; at best, they can accomplish specific things in the context of continuing international political conflict.

In concrete terms, this means that the first step must be to rewrite and substantially narrow the arms control agenda. What is needed most is a clear set of priorities: a firm sense of what is important and what is trivial. Even in its early days, the experience of the Carter administration demonstrated conclusively that neither the American political system nor the contemporary condition of relations among nations is capable of sustaining arms negotiations on a broad front. Some of the Carter administration initiatives conflicted with one another substantively. All competed with one another both for the attention of high-level decision-makers and for the political capital necessary to move them through a resistant bureaucracy and equally difficult international system.

The next administration, Republican or Democratic, must decide what is important and what is feasible and pursue limitations only in those few areas. Policymakers must be ruthless in this regard. There is a tendency to accept new objectives even when their prospects are perceived to be hopeless, as a means of pleasing constituents with actions that are considered harmless. In fact, however, the larding of the arms control agenda with foolish initiatives demeans those items which are significant, wasting time and influence, and casting a naïve pall over the entire policy, regardless of the intrinsic merits of specific items.

For convenience, the prospective arms control agenda can be divided into three main areas: arms control in Europe, U.S.-Soviet negotiations on nuclear weapons, and multilateral arms control.

Arms Control in Europe. The politico-military situation in Europe comes closest to the conditions necessary for the success of arms negotiations. East-West political and economic relations in Europe are relatively cooperative, and have been that way for more than ten years. With a few obvious exceptions, political systems on both sides of the demarcation line are stable; most economies are doing reasonably well. Ties between the two halves of Europe continue to deepen and to expand in scope. The fact that, so far at least, détente in Europe has survived the deterioration of U.S.-Soviet relations demonstrates the stability of the situation.

European political leaders in both East and West have considerable incentive to ensure that things do not change. Détente has a tangible economic meaning in Europe which it never gained in the United States. Détente also has a very human dimension for Europeans, as it facilitates exchanges, such as family visits, across the boundary between East and West. For East Europeans, détente has meant a relaxation of political and economic restrictions. The threat of war, which would rise quickly if Europe returned to more tense East-West relations, also has a more pointed historic meaning for Europeans than for most Americans. And, not insignificantly, West European nations—for the most part—are ruled by individuals who partly have built their careers on rapprochement, and by political parties whose ideologies stress the need for international cooperation.

Despite all this, the East-West military competition in Europe continues to escalate. Both sides are now substantially expanding their military capabilities on the continent. The Warsaw Pact, particularly in its Soviet component, grew somewhat in size and began to accelerate its equipment modernization more than ten years ago. NATO responded slowly, but is now taking important steps to expand its combat capabilities, by raising force levels slightly and sharply accelerating its modernization programs, as well as taking other steps to improve the efficiency with which the alliance as a whole makes use of its members' contributions. The nations of NATO now seem resolved to increase their military spending beyond the amount necessary to offset inflation each year. Over time, given NATO's far greater resource base, this would reverse the past trend in relative capabilities between East and West.

These continuing military buildups have an adverse effect on the political situation in Europe. At a minimum, they delay and make more difficult the strengthening of détente. More likely, over time—by contributing to a diffuse sense of unease and apprehension—they can actually erode the progress made in the past, thus contributing to new tensions and a greater risk of war. At times, specific decisions can have more pointed and immediate political effects, as in the case of the Soviet deployment of ss-20 mobile intermediate-range missiles and the resultant NATO decision to deploy both a new-model ballistic missile and ground-launched cruise missiles capable of striking Soviet territory. Should certain contingencies occur, whether civil strife in Yugoslavia, turmoil in Poland, or anarchy in Italy, the suspicions and concerns resulting from the continuing momentum of the military competition can make the avoidance of military conflict more difficult. Overall, it seems doubtful that political stability and détente can survive indefinitely in the face of unbridled military competition.

This is an excellent opportunity for arms control. Theoretically at least, given the relatively benign political situation, it should be possible to negotiate mutual limitations on the military forces of the two sides which can dampen these adverse consequences of continuing military deployments. Such negotiations would not erase the remaining differences between East and West but, potentially, they could confine the degree to which the military competition independently aggravates the political situation. They would not end the need for NATO to respond to the Soviet military buildup but, by confining growth in Soviet capabilities, they could moderate the burden of defense in the West.

There are three potential forums for such negotiations: the now seven-year-old NATO-Warsaw Pact talks in Vienna for mutual and balanced force reductions (MBFR) in central

Europe; the Conference on Security and Cooperation in Europe (CSCE), which previously negotiated and incorporated in the Helsinki Final Act certain measures to increase the confidence with which each side was able to view the other's military activities, and for which a review conference is scheduled to begin in Madrid in November of 1980; and the French proposal for a Conference on Disarmament in Europe (CDE), which has received some support from both the Warsaw Pact and the West Germans.

If these putative negotiations are each pursued separately, they are all virtually guaranteed either to fail or to produce insignificant results. Progress toward arms control in Europe requires a unified approach with the support of all members of both blocs, as well as the neutral and nonaligned states. Seemingly most promising would be a strategy that sought to terminate the MBFR talks with completion of the proposal now on the table—calling chiefly for modest asymmetrical reductions in military personnel—and then moved to assimilate the French CDE proposal within the CSCE context.

MBFR is badly flawed by its limited geographic scope, its too-long history, its endless debates over data, the refusal of the French to participate, and, most important, its emphasis on bloc-to-bloc confrontation. The talks have served some useful purposes—mainly, perhaps, in terms of their effects on intra-NATO consultations and procedures—but have outlived their usefulness. They require some sort of modest agreement to permit a graceful exit for all parties. The proposal put on the table by the West in December would provide an equitable, if essentially symbolic, agreement, and a convenient way to end the talks. It is now up to the U.S.S.R. to respond so as to complete the negotiation.

In the meantime, the preliminary steps necessary to fuse the CSCE and CDE concepts and inaugurate the new negotiating forum could be taken at the CSCE Review Conference. It may be possible at Madrid, in fact, to make more stringent the confidence-building measures already included in the Helsinki Final Act. More important, however, would be the creation of a CSCE working group on European security issues. Such a group could incorporate the essence of the French CDE proposal—addressing the broad definition of Europe (from the Urals to the Atlantic) and shifting from bloc-to-bloc to true multinational negotiations; the group might even meet in Paris. At the outset it might take up a number of additional confidence-building measures. If these negotiations proved successful, the talks could shift to the tougher issues of quantitative limitations on conventional forces.

U.S.-Soviet Negotiations on Strategic Weapons. The SALT II treaty obviously is gravely wounded. It has had such a difficult history, it is associated in a large part of the public's mind with such negative events, its politics are so bad—that any new administration, including a second Carter administration, would be reluctant to enter yet again into the maelstrom of congressional debate on the treaty. Yet the treaty will not disappear; some action will have to be taken, and the character of that action will have an important impact on U.S.-Soviet relations. The test will come early in 1981. The U.S. elections will be past; presumably, U.S.-Soviet relations will have stabilized, even if, as is likely, they entail a high level of tension and open political conflict.

Under such conditions, there would be important reasons to seek to preserve the terms of SALT II. It is precisely at the times when U.S.-Soviet confrontation is most acute that the benefits of SALT are most significant. Confrontational politics seem likely to be the watchword for at least the next several years. Reducing the nuclear component of the risks associated with such a situation could be a crucial plus.

Besides, the treaty places significant limitations on Soviet strategic forces. It restricts the number of warheads on Soviet missiles and the number of such missiles themselves. It retards modernization of Soviet land-based missiles. The pace and status of Soviet strategic programs is such that these provisions could be violated rapidly once the Kremlin decided that SALT was either dead or undesirable. Most Americans now agree that the United States must take major steps to improve its own strategic capabilities. These steps will take time, however. The treaty confines Soviet options at precisely the time when the United States would be most disadvantaged, the period between now and 1985. In the absence of SALT II's constraints on Soviet programs, the United States may be playing catch-up for far longer than is now contemplated, regardless of the size of the step-up in our own efforts.

Whether these considerations will be persuasive remains to be seen. The immediate need is for both sides to avoid steps that violate the terms of the treaty. If such a tacit agreement can be maintained until 1981, it may be possible to consider resubmitting the treaty to the Congress. Conceivably, the two sides might find it in their mutual interest to make some minor changes to the treaty, changes sufficient to take the political curse off the present document. Alternatively, it could be possible to devise some procedural arrangement to maintain tacit observance of the treaty while negotiations are reopened on a new agreement. There will always be a temptation in the United States, particularly if a new administration takes office, to throw away SALT II and begin again. That temptation should be avoided. In one sense, SALT's current problems stem from this administration's initial decision to discard the Vladivostok accord in favor of something better.

Beyond SALT II, questions about the future of the ABM treaty will recur. The key date is 1982—the year of the next scheduled review conference. Unquestionably, pressure will mount to scrap or at least to amend the treaty significantly. These pressures will be greater if SALT II is not preserved, but they will exist regardless, in view of new developments in relevant technologies, the ostensible potential of ABMS to facilitate the deployment of survivable land-based offensive missile systems, and the blood already drawn by some opponents of SALT—whose real target has always been the ABM treaty and its implications for U.S.-Soviet relations. Determining one's position on the question of whether the ABM treaty should or should not be amended requires evaluation of the potential benefits and costs of the new technologies, a comparable survey of alternative methods of accomplishing similar ends, and a political assessment of the consequences of seeking to revise one of the few major accomplishments of arms negotiations.

If SALT II continues to be observed, formally or informally, and if the ABM treaty is preserved, even if modified to permit defense of additional ICBM sites, consideration of the style and substance of new negotiations on offensive weapons may again become relevant. Too much must occur between now and then, however, and too much ink has already been futilely spilled on the subject of SALT III, to warrant such speculation at present.

In the interim, the U.S.-Soviet Standing Consultative Commission, a confidential body established by the ABM treaty, could provide a useful forum for continued discussions of the modalities of U.S. and Soviet behavior that could best preserve what progress has been made in the past, as well as options for the future if political relations thaw. These talks could touch on what is necessary to preserve the "objectives and purposes" of SALT II, the beginnings of a dialogue on the question of whether to revise the ABM treaty, and, conceivably, the types of national behavior that could most support chances for a future agreement to prevent the escalation of U.S.-Soviet military competition in space.

Multilateral Arms Control. There clearly must be a shift in emphasis from bilateral U.S.-Soviet negotiations to multilateral forums. There has been a tendency to seek U.S.-Soviet agreement as a first step, believing that once that nut had been cracked, wider agreement would follow. This has not only placed undue burdens on U.S.-Soviet relations, but has nurtured the fears of those who see arms control as an expression of U.S.-Soviet condominium, thereby aggravating the political problems already surrounding the negotiations.

Problems more appropriately tackled in multilateral, rather than bilateral, forums include those of nuclear tests, chemical weapons, and arms sales. These phenomena pose dangers to the security of all, not just the citizens of the United States and the Soviet Union. There is no reason why the United States should place itself in the position of *demandeur* on these matters, as is implied when it takes initiatives for U.S.-Soviet agreements preliminary to multilateral solutions. Indeed, unnecessary problems are often created when it appears that the superpowers are dictating the terms of agreement to less powerful nations, a problem faced, for example, in the recent talks to restrain arms sales.

The multilateral forum most appropriate for these discussions is the U.N.'s Committee on Disarmament. Recently reorganized, the Committee now includes all the nuclear powers, as China took its seat during the spring 1980 session. The United States can and should play a constructive role within the Committee, but its posture should be relatively low key. Separate U.S.-Soviet discussions might take place, at times, as on the details of additional protocols to aid verification arrangements, but these talks should be viewed as complementary, not as substitutes for discussions in the Committee or any working groups that it establishes. Moreover, such separate talks need not take place until it is clear that multilateral agreement is feasible. Some will argue that this proposal condemns these negotiations to failure. But the substantive problems that make multilateral negotiations difficult—for example, the reluctance of some nuclear powers to end nuclear testing—would not disappear even if the United States and the U.S.S.R. could reach agreement. Moreover, the faltering bilateral talks further impede other forms of U.S.-Soviet cooperation.

Others will fear that greater emphasis on the Committee on Disarmament would put pressure on the United States to subscribe to agreements that it would otherwise prefer to avoid. That argument too is spurious. There is no substantive reason why the United States, like France, could not persist in defense of its own perception of proper approaches to, and necessary conditions for, arms control, including—wherever appropriate—a firm insistence that any agreements include adequate attention to verification.

V

Judged by the standards of the recent past, this agenda is modest in the extreme. Yet what is needed now—and

badly—are tangible accomplishments. After 20 years of gran-
diose declarations, absolute objectives, ambitious agendas and
inspiring speeches, we need results—pragmatic steps toward
the limitation of arms.

If negotiated arms limitations are to have a future, they
need to return to the more limited concept which originally
characterized arms control. In this heterogeneous world of
sovereign nations, there are real conflicts—over land, over
economic rights, over religious and political values. And there
are real villains in this world as well—individuals dedicated
to the aggrandizement of themselves, their friends, their nations, even at the expense of others, and even at grave risk of
war. Weapons are not the cause of these conflicts, they are
their reflection. Discussions about weapons cannot solve these
conflicts; they can—and even then only at certain times—
contain their effects.

In another sense, given the rhetoric of confrontation which
now characterizes U.S.-Soviet exchanges, even this modest
agenda may appear naïve. An acceptance of a return to more
tense U.S.-Soviet relations, however, need not include the
abandonment of efforts to contain the military competition at
its most dangerous points. Given the extraordinary uncertainties of nuclear war and the unprecedented potential of
nuclear weapons for destruction, containing the effects of
political conflict, reducing the risk of war—even if only
modestly—could be a crucial accomplishment. The effort
deserves our attention, and it also requires our support.

ARMS CONTROL FOR THE 1980s: AN AMERICAN POLICY[2]

I do want to say I'm very, very pleased to have an opportunity to talk again before the Foreign Policy Association.

[2] Excerpts from an address by Secretary of State Alexander M. Haig before the
Foreign Policy Association in New York on July 14, 1981. *Department of State
Bulletin.* 80:31–4. Ag. '81.

I've always believed that an effective policy abroad must be the product of support for that policy here at home. And this association and its activities have clearly made a major contribution to that requirement here in America. It has always sharpened the issues for the American people and enabled them to decide for themselves on these fundamental issues. And it is just such an issue that I would like to discuss today ... the future of arms control in this decade of the 1980s ... There is hardly a subject which enjoys or is a focus of greater international attention, especially recently, among our allies in Western Europe, and with good cause.

This is true because we are living in an age when man has conceived the means of his own destruction. The supreme interest of the United States has been to avoid the extremes of either nuclear catastrophe or nuclear blackmail. Beginning with the Baruch plan, every President has sought international agreement to control nuclear weapons and to prevent their proliferation. But each Chief Executive has also recognized that our national security and the security of our allies depend on American nuclear forces as well.

President Reagan stands in this tradition. He understands the dangers of unchecked nuclear arms. He shares the universal aspiration for a more secure and peaceful world. But he also shares the universal disappointment that the arms control process has delivered less than it has promised.

One of the President's first acts was to order an intense review of arms control policy, the better to learn the lessons of the past in the hope of achieving more lasting progress for the future. Two fundamental conclusions have emerged from this review.

First, the search for sound arms control agreements should be an essential element of our program for achieving and maintaining peace.

Second, such agreements can be reached if negotiations among adversaries about their national security interests are not dominated by pious hopes and simplistic solutions.

The task of arms control is enormously complex. It must be related to the nation's security needs and perspectives.

Above all, arms control policy must be seen in the light of international realities. As Churchill put it: "You must look at the facts because they look at you." An American arms control policy for this decade must take into account the facts about our security and the lessons that we have learned about what works—and what does not work—in arms control.

Despite the extraordinary efforts at arms control during the 1970s, the world is a less secure place than it was 10 years ago. We began the process with the expectation that it would help to secure the deterrent forces of both the United States and the Soviet Union. But Moscow's strategic buildup has put at risk both our crucial land-based missiles and our bombers. Simultaneously, the Soviets have continued a massive buildup of conventional forces and have used them with increasing boldness. Their armies and those of their surrogates have seized positions that threaten resources and routes critical to Western security.

We cannot blame our approach to arms control alone for our failure to restrain the growth and use of Soviet power. The Soviet Union did not feel compelled to agree to major limitations and adequate verification in part because the United States did not take steps needed to maintain its own strategic and conventional capabilities. Nor did we respond vigorously to the use of Soviet force. The turmoil of the 1960s, Vietnam, and Watergate all contributed to this passivity. As a result, the basis for arms control was undermined. We overestimated the extent to which the Strategic Arms Limitation Talks would help to ease other tensions. We also underestimated the impact that such tensions would have on the arms control process itself.

This experience teaches us that arms control can only be one element in a comprehensive structure of defense and foreign policy designed to reduce the risks of war. It cannot be the political centerpiece or the crucial barometer of U.S.-Soviet relationships, burdening arms control with a crushing political weight. It can hardly address such issues as the Soviet invasion of Afghanistan, the Iran-Iraq war, the Vietnamese invasion of Kampuchea—which is the subject of our U.N.

conference here this week—the Libyan invasion of Chad, or Cuban intervention in Africa and Latin America. Instead, arms control should be an element—a single element—in a full range of political, economic, and military efforts to promote peace and security.

Principles

The lessons of history and the facts of international life provide the basis for a realistic set of principles to guide a more effective approach to arms control. All of our principles are derived from a recognition that the paramount aim of arms control must be to reduce the risks of war. We owe it to ourselves and to posterity to follow principles wedded exclusively to that aim.

Our first principle is that our arms control efforts will be an instrument of, not a replacement for, a coherent allied security policy. Arms control proposals should be designed in the context of the security situation we face, our military needs, and our defense strategy. Arms control should complement military programs in meeting these needs. Close consultation with our allies is an essential part of this process, both to protect their interests and to strengthen the Western position in negotiations with the Soviet Union.

If, conversely, we make our defense programs dependent on progress in arms control, then we will give the Soviets a veto over our defenses and remove their incentive to negotiate fair arrangements. Should we expect Moscow to respect parity if we demonstrate that we are not prepared to sacrifice to sustain it? Can we expect the Soviets to agree to limitations if they realize that, in the absence of agreement, we shall not match their efforts? In the crucial relationship between arms and arms control, we must not put the cart before the horse. There is little prospect of agreements with the Soviet Union that will help solve such a basic security problem as the vulnerability of our land-based missiles until we demonstrate that we have the will and the capacity to solve them without arms control, should that be necessary.

Our second principle is that we will seek arms control agreements that truly enhance security. We will work for agreements that make world peace more secure by reinforcing deterrence. On occasion it has been urged that we accept defective agreements in order "to keep the arms control process alive." But we are seeking much more than agreements for their own sake. We will design our proposals not simply in the interest of a speedy negotiation but so that they will result in agreements which genuinely enhance the security of both sides.

That is the greatest measure of the worth of arms control, not the money saved nor the arms eliminated. Indeed, valuable agreements can be envisioned that do not save money and that do not eliminate arms. The vital task is to limit and to reduce arms in a way that renders the use of the remaining arms less likely.

Just as arms control could not aim simply at reducing numbers, so it should not try simply to restrict the advance of technology. Some technological advances make everyone safer. Reconnaissance satellites, for instance, discourage surprise attacks by increasing warning and make verification of agreements possible. Submarines and other means of giving mobility to strategic systems enhance their survivability, reduce the advantage of preemptive strikes, and thus help to preserve the peace. Our proposals will take account of both the positive and the negative effects of advancing technology.

Whether a particular weapons system, and therefore a particular agreement, undermines or supports deterrence may change with the development of other weapons systems. At one time, fixed intercontinental ballistic missiles (ICBMs) were a highly stable form of strategic weapons deployments, but technological change has altered that. We need to design arms control treaties so that they can adapt flexibly to long-term changes. A treaty that, for example, had the effect of locking us into fixed ICBM deployments would actually detract from the objectives of arms control.

Our third principle is that we will seek arms control bearing in mind the whole context of Soviet conduct worldwide.

Escalation of a crisis produced by Soviet aggression could lead to a nuclear war, particularly if we allowed an imbalance of forces to provide an incentive for a Soviet first strike. American foreign policy and defense policy, of which arms control is one element, must deter aggression, contain crisis, reduce sources of conflict, and achieve a more stable military balance—all for the purpose of securing the peace. These tasks cannot be undertaken successfully in isolation one from the other.

Soviet international conduct directly affects the prospects for success in arms control. Recognition of this reality is essential for a healthy arms control process in the long run. Such "linkage" is not the creation of U.S. policy: It is a fact of life. A policy of pretending that there is no linkage promotes reverse linkage. It ends up by saying that in order to preserve arms control, we have to tolerate Soviet aggression. This Administration will never accept such an appalling conclusion.

Our fourth principle is that we will seek balanced arms control agreements. Balanced agreements are necessary for a relationship based on reciprocity and essential to maintaining the security of both sides. The Soviet Union must be more willing in the future to accept genuine parity for arms control to move ahead. Each agreement must be balanced in itself and contribute to an overall balance.

Quantitative parity is important, but balance is more than a matter of numbers. One cannot always count different weapons systems as if they were equivalent. What matters is the capacity of either side to make decisive gains through military operations or threat of military operations. Agreements that do not effectively reduce the incentives to use force, especially in crisis situations, do nothing at all to enhance security.

Our fifth principle is that we will seek arms controls that include effective means of verification and mechanisms for securing compliance. Unverifiable agreements only increase uncertainties, tensions, and risks. The critical obstacle in virtually every area of arms control in the 1970s was Soviet unwillingness to accept the verification measures needed for more ambitious limitations. As much as any other single factor, whether the Soviets are forthcoming on this question will determine the degree of progress in arms contrcl in the 1980s.

Failure of the entire arms control process in the long run can be avoided only if compliance issues are clearly resolved. For example, there have been extremely disturbing reports of the use of chemical weapons by the Soviets or their proxies in Afghanistan and in Southeast Asia. With full Western support the United Nations is now investigating the issue of chemical weapons. Similarly, in the spring of 1979, there was an extraordinary outbreak of anthrax in the Soviet city of Sverdlovsk. Despite continued probing, we still await a serious Soviet explanation as to whether it was linked to activities prohibited under the biological weapons convention.

Our sixth principle is that our strategy must consider the totality of the various arms control processes and various weapons systems, not only those that are being specifically negotiated. Each U.S. weapons system must be understood not merely in connection with a corresponding Soviet system, but in relation to our whole strategy for deterring the Soviets from exploiting military force in general. In developing our theater nuclear arms control proposals, for example, we should consider the relationship of theater nuclear forces to NATO's overall strategy for deterring war in Europe. We cannot overlook the fact that our European strategy has always compensated for shortfalls in conventional capability through a greater reliance on theater and strategic nuclear forces. If we are to rely less on the nuclear elements in the future, the conventional elements will have to be strengthened.

Prospects

What then are the prospects for arms control in the 1980s? We could achieve quick agreements and an appearance of progress if we pursued negotiation for its own sake or for the political symbolism of continuing the process. But we are committed to serious arms control that truly strengthens international security. That is why our approach must be prudent, paced, and measured.

With a clear sense of direction and a dedication to the serious objectives of arms control, this Administration will strive to make arms control succeed. We will put our principles into action. We will conduct negotiations based on close consultation with our allies, guided by the understanding that our objective is enhanced security for all of our allies, not just for the United States. We will work with the Congress to insure that our arms control proposals reflect the desires of our people, and that, once agreements are negotiated, they will be ratified and their implementation fully supported. We will comply with agreements we make, and we will demand that others do likewise.

By the end of the year, the United States will be embarked upon a new arms control endeavor of fundamental importance, one designed to reduce the Soviet nuclear threat to our European allies. The impetus for these negotiations dates back to the mid-1970s when the Soviets began producing and deploying a whole new generation of nuclear systems designed not to threaten the United States—for their range was too short—but to threaten our European allies. These new weapons, and in particular the nearly 3,000-mile-range SS-20 missile, were not just modernized replacements for older systems. Because of their much greater range, their mobility, and above all their multiplication of warheads on each missile, these new systems presented the alliance with a threat of a new order of magnitude.

The pace of the Soviet buildup is increasing. Since the beginning of last year, the Soviets have more than doubled their SS-20 force. Already 750 warheads have been deployed on SS-20 launchers. The Soviet Union has continued to deploy the long-range Backfire bomber and a whole array of new medium- and short-range nuclear missiles and nuclear-capable aircraft. This comprehensive Soviet arms buildup is in no sense a reaction to NATO's defense program. Indeed, NATO did very little as this alarming buildup progressed.

In December 1979, the alliance finally responded in two ways. First, it agreed to deploy 464 new U.S. ground-launched cruise missiles in Europe and to replace 108 medium-range Pershing ballistic missiles already located there with modernized versions of greater range. Second, the alliance agreed that the United States should pursue negotiated limits on U.S. and Soviet systems in this category.

This two-track decision represents explicit recognition that arms control cannot succeed unless it is matched by a clear determination to take the defense measures necessary to restore a secure balance. On taking office, as one of its first foreign policy initiatives, this Administration announced its commitment to both tracks of the alliance decision—deployments and arms control. . . .

Extensive preliminary preparations for this entirely new area of arms control are already underway in Washington and in consultation with our NATO allies in Brussels. Senior U.S. and European officials will continue to consult after the beginning of U.S.-Soviet exchanges. We and our allies recognize that progress can only come through complex, extensive, and intensive negotiations.

We approach these negotiations with a clear sense of purpose. We want equal, verifiable limits on the lowest possible level on U.S. and Soviet theater nuclear forces. Such limits would reduce the threat to our allies and bring to Europe the security undermined today by the Soviet buildup. We regard the threat to our allies as a threat to ourselves, and we will, therefore, spare no effort to succeed.

We are proceeding with these negotiations to limit the theater threat within the framework of SALT—the Strategic Arms Limitation Talks designed to limit the nuclear threat to the United States and to the Soviet Union. In this area, too, we have initiated intense preparations. These preparations must take into account the decisions we will take shortly on modernizing our intercontinental ballistic missiles and our strategic bombers.

In the course of 10 years of SALT negotiations, conceptual questions have arisen which must be addressed. For instance, how have improvements in monitoring capabilities, on the one hand, and new possibilities for deception and concealment, on the other, affected our ability to verify agreements and to improve verification? Which systems are to be included in a SALT negotiation, and which should be discussed in other forums? How can we compare and limit the diverse U.S. and Soviet military arsenals in the light of new systems and new technologies emerging on both sides?

In each of these areas there are serious and pressing questions which must be answered to insure the progress of SALT in the 1980s and beyond. Only in this way can SALT become again a dynamic process that will promote greater security in the U.S.-Soviet relationship. We are determined to solve these problems and to do everything necessary to arrive at balanced reductions in strategic arsenals on both sides.

We should be prepared to pursue innovative arms control ideas. For example, negotiated confidence-building measures in Europe could provide a valuable means to reduce uncertainty about the character and purpose of the other side's military activities. While measures of this sort will not lessen the imperative of maintaining a military balance in Europe, they can reduce the dangers of miscalculation and surprise.

We are eager to pursue such steps in the framework of a European disarmament conference based on an important French proposal now being considered at the Madrid meeting of the Conference on Security and Cooperation in Europe. We call upon the Soviets to accept this proposal, which could cover Soviet territory to the Urals. As we proceed in Madrid, we will do so on the basis of a firm alliance solidarity, which is the key to bringing the Soviets to accept serious and effective arms control measures.

Our efforts to control existing nuclear arsenals will be accompanied by new attempts to prevent the spread of nuclear weapons. The Reagan Administration is developing more vigorous policies for inhibiting nuclear proliferation. We expect the help of others in this undertaking, and we intend to be a more forthcoming partner to those who share responsibility for nonproliferation practices. Proliferation complicates the task of arms control: It increases the risk of preemptive and accidental war, it detracts from the maintenance of a stable balance of conventional forces, and it brings weapons of unparalleled destructiveness to volatile and developing regions. No short-term gain in export revenue or regional prestige can be worth such risks.

It may be argued that the "genie is out of the bottle," that technology is already out of control. But technology can also be tapped for the answers. Our policies can diminish the insecurities that motivate proliferation. Responsible export practices can reduce dangers. And international norms can increase the cost of nuclear violations. With effort we can help to assure that nuclear plowshares are not transformed into nuclear swords.

In sum, the United States has a broad agenda of specific arms control efforts and negotiations already underway or soon to be launched. The charge that we are not interested in arms control or that we have cut off communications with the Soviets on these issues is simply not true.

The approach I have discussed today stands in a long and distinguished American tradition. We are confident that it is a serious and realistic approach to the enduring problems of arms control. The United States wants a more secure and a more peaceful world. And we know that balanced, verifiable arms control can contribute to that objective.

We are also confident that the Soviet leaders will realize the seriousness of our intent. They should soon tire of the proposals that seek to freeze NATO's modernization of theater nuclear weapons before it has even begun, while reserving for themselves the advantages of hundreds of SS-20s already deployed. They should see that the propaganda campaign intended to intimidate our allies and frustrate NATO's modernization program cannot and must not succeed. Arms control requires confidence, but it also requires patience. . . .

It is one of the paradoxes of our time that the prospects for arms control depend upon the achievement of a balance of arms. We seek to negotiate a balance at less dangerous levels but meanwhile we must maintain our strength. Let us take to heart John F. Kennedy's reminder that negotiations "are not a substitute for strength—they are an instrument for the translation of strength into survival and peace."

WHITE HOUSE STATEMENT ON PROGRAMS FOR B-1 BOMBER AND MX MISSILE[3]

Overview
Introduction

Over the past few months, we have developed a comprehensive plan for revitalizing our strategic deterrent.

This program will end the relative decline of U.S. strategic competition in the years ahead.

Objectives of Program

The Reagan program will, within the next four to eight years, redress the most serious weaknesses in our current posture.

Communications and control systems will be improved to make sure we could communicate with our strategic forces, even after a nuclear attack.

Our triad of land-based ballistic missiles, bombers and sea-based missiles will be strengthened and modernized as soon as possible, ending long-standing delays in some of these programs.

The Reagan program will determine, to a large extent, U.S. strategic capabilities into the next century. Not since the Eisenhower years has an administration proposed a nuclear program of such breadth and scope.

We have used this unique opportunity to mold a strategic force that will meet the objectives of our strategy and serve as a coherent instrument of national policy.

[3] Reprint of the text of a background statement by the White House on programs for the B-1 Bomber and MX Missile. Released by the White House October 2, 1981.

The Reagan program will create a deterrent to Soviet action against us that is far more secure and stable than exists today.

The Reagan program will increase Soviet incentives to negotiate genuine arms reductions. And, if we must, the proposed program will put us in a good position to strengthen our forces further in response to unconstrained growth in Soviet weapons.

5 Elements of Program

There are five mutually reinforcing elements of the Reagan program:

Improvements in communications and control systems.

Modernization of strategic bombers.

Deployment of new submarine-launched missiles.

A step-by-step plan to improve the strength and accuracy of new land-based missiles, and to reduce their vulnerability.

Improvements in strategic defenses.

Each of these elements will be discussed in more detail in the following pages.

Capabilities and Cost of Program

The Reagan program stresses survivability and endurance.

Compared with today's forces, we will, by 1990, roughly double the number of U.S. strategic weapons that could survive a Soviet nuclear attack on our country.

We will be able to communicate with these forces during an attack, immediately following an attack, and, if necessary, for extended periods afterwards.

These improvements will greatly strengthen deterrence of nuclear war by denying the Soviets any realistic prospects, however they may define them, of gaining an advantage by initiating the use of nuclear weapons.

The Reagan strategic program is affordable; it fits within the fiscal guidelines announced recently by the President.

In the early 1960s, when we built many of the nuclear

forces that still exist today, the U.S. spent over 20% of the total defense budget on strategic forces.

Now, as we modernize our entire arsenal, we anticipate spending less than 15% of the defense budget on strategic forces in each of the next five years.

To help fund new initiatives, some obsolescent forces will be retired, with little effect on overall capabilities.

Thus, we plan to modernize strategic forces and still meet our other commitments, including strengthening the rapid deployment force, enhancing conventional and theater nuclear capabilities in Europe, expanding our naval and air power worldwide, and insuring that our armed forces have an adequate supply of well-trained men and women.

Communications and Control
Systems
Description

We will improve the survivability, performance and coverage of radars and satellites used to warn us of a Soviet missile attack and to assess its size and scope.

Mobile ground terminals for processing data from our warning satellites will be deployed, and the satellites themselves will be upgraded to improve survivability.

Warning satellites and ground-based radars will be improved to give better estimates of the size and objectives of a Soviet missile attack.

Additional PAVE PAWS surveillance radars will be deployed to improve coverage of potential Soviet submarine operating areas to the southeast and southwest of the United States.

We plan to upgrade the survivability and capability of command centers that would direct U.S. strategic forces during a nuclear war.

E-4B airborne command posts will be deployed to serve the National Command Authority in time of war.

EC-135 airborne command posts serving military commanders will be hardened against nuclear effects and will be equipped with upgraded satellite and very low frequency-low frequency communications.

We will deploy survivable communications that link command centers with all three legs of the triad.

Very low frequency-low frequency communications receivers will be developed and installed on strategic bombers to insure their reception of orders.

We will upgrade communications to deployed submarines.

A new satellite communications system will be developed providing extremely high frequency communication channels that would insure two-way communications between commanders and forces.

We will initiate a vigorous and comprehensive R & D (research and development) program leading to a communications and control system that would endure for an extended period beyond the first nuclear attack.

Reasons for Program

Strategic communications and control systems are needed to insure that we could employ our nuclear forces effectively, which is essential to a credible deterrent.

Timely warning would be needed to insure survivability of our alert forces; assessment of the attack would be needed to select an appropriate U.S. response.

Mobile command centers that could survive an initial attack would be needed to insure that we have the means to direct a retaliation, even if our fixed command centers were destroyed.

Survivable communications links would be needed to insure the reliable dissemination of orders to our ICBMs, bombers and submarines.

Over the past decade, we have not modernized communications and control systems fast enough. As a result, these systems are not as survivable as we would like, and they could not operate reliably over an extended period after a Soviet attack, if that proved to be necessary.

The Reagan program will significantly improve the survivability and endurance of strategic communications and control systems. These improved systems will be as strong as the modernized forces they support.

Bomber Program
Description

We plan to develop a variant of the B-1 bomber and deploy 100 aircraft. The first squadron of B-1s will be operational in 1986.

We will continue a vigorous R & D program for an advanced technology bomber (the so-called "Stealth" aircraft). This bomber, under current plans, will be deployed in the 1990s.

Newer B-52s (G and H models) will be modified to carry cruise missiles. Selected aircraft will be modernized to provide added protection against the effects of nuclear explosions (particularly electromagnetic pulse effects) and to improve their ability to survive against Soviet air defenses (by installation of additional electronic counter-measures equipment). Older B-52s (D model) will be retired in 1982 and 1983.

Over 3,000 cruise missiles will be deployed on B-52Gs, B-52Hs and B-1s. The first squadron of cruise missile-equipped aircraft (B-52Gs) will be operational in 1982.

Existing KC-135 aerial tankers will be outfitted with new engines to increase airborne refueling capabilities.

Reasons for 2 Types of New Bombers

There is a general consensus on the need for new strategic bombers. The only issues are which bombers to build and when.

The previous administration planned to rely on B-52s in the 1980s and to develop the advanced technology bomber for the 1990s.

This represented a willingness to accept risks associated with an aging and potentially vulnerable B-52 force and risks associated with the uncertain schedule and unproven capabilities of the advanced technology bomber.

The Reagan administration believes the B-1 is necessary to bolster our strategic forces during the critical 1980s, and the advanced technology bomber is needed to provide high confidence that our bombers will be able to penetrate Soviet air defenses into the next century.

The U.S. must depend heavily on bombers (and sea-based forces) in the 1980s while we take steps to strengthen our land-based missiles. We can't afford to wait until the 1990s for a new bomber.

The B-1 will be available in significant numbers by 1987 in accordance with the congressional mandate; the advanced technology bomber will not be available until the 1990s. Building the B-1 will allow time to develop an advanced technology bomber that really works.

There are currently technical and operational uncertainties about the advanced technology bomber. We believe these uncertainties will be resolved during development and that the advanced technology bomber will be a very effective aircraft when ultimately deployed.

Without the B-1, however, there would be pressures to accelerate the advanced technology bomber, which would increase program risks and possibly result in a less capable aircraft being deployed.

Building two bombers will stimulate competition and give the Defense Department the flexibility to adjust bomber procurement in accordance with any changes in estimates of the cost and effectiveness of the two aircraft.

The B-1 will be able to penetrate Soviet defenses initially and will make a good cruise missile carrier and conventional bomber after the advanced technology bomber is deployed and all B-52s are retired in the 1990s.

If we did not build the B-1 now, we would have to start development of another aircraft in the late 1980s or early 1990s to replace B-52s as cruise missile carriers.

Thus, over the long run, we would not save much money, and we would postpone once more the deployment of a needed modernization program.

Sea-Based Forces
Description

We plan to continue construction of Trident ballistic missile submarines at a steady rate of one per year, including one submarine in 1981 (the contract is under negotiation), one submarine in 1982 (partially funded in the F.Y. 82 budget, the remainder will be funded in the F.Y. 83 budget), and one submarine per year in 1983 to 1987.

We will develop a larger and more accurate, sea-launched ballistic missile, known as the Trident II or D-5 missile, for deployment on Trident submarines beginning in 1989.

We will deploy several hundred nuclear-armed sea-launched cruise missiles on general purpose submarines beginning in 1984.

Reasons for Program

Sea-based forces currently represent the most survivable leg of our strategic triad. The Reagan program expands and further strengthens these forces.

The new D-5 missile will carry more warheads and or larger ones than current C-4 submarine-launched missiles, nearly doubling the capability of each Trident submarine.

By increasing the payload of each Trident, we will be able to avoid a reduction in sea-based capabilities when large numbers of existing Poseidon submarines reach the end of their service lives and must be retired in the 1990s.

The new D-5 missile will also have much better accuracy than current sea-based missiles. They will allow us to use sea-launched missiles to attack any target in the Soviet Union, including their missile silos.

To deploy highly accurate nuclear warheads at sea in the near term, we plan to put cruise missiles on existing attack submarines. These missiles will be particularly valuable as a strategic reserve force, a key part of our deterrent posture.

Deployment of nuclear sea-launched cruise missiles to strengthen our strategic reserve and to deter the use of nu-

clear weapons against our naval forces worldwide does not
diminish the critical need to deploy ground-launched cruise
missiles and the Pershing II ballistic missile to counter
the massive Soviet buildup of theater nuclear forces in
Europe.

ICBM Modernization
Description

The so-called multiple protective shelter basing scheme
for the MX missile will be canceled.

We will continue to develop MX and deploy at least 100
missiles.

We will pursue R & D on three promising long-term, basing options for MX. The development programs will be
structured to allow us to select for deployment one or more of
these options by 1984:

Continuous Airborne Patrol Aircraft. A survivable long-
endurance aircraft that could launch MX.

Ballistic Missile Defense. Active defense of land-based
MX missiles.

Deep Underground Basing. Deployment of MX in survivable locations deep underground.

In the near term, we will deploy a limited number of MX
missiles, as soon as possible, in Titan and Minuteman silos that
will be reconstructed for much greater hardness to nuclear
effects.

Although specific base locations are still under review, the
most likely site for the initial MX deployment is an existing
Titan base.

All aging Titan missiles will be deactivated as soon as possible.

Reasons for Changing the MX Program

The previous administration planned to conceal MX by
moving the missiles among thousands of relatively soft shel-

ters in Utah and Nevada (multiple protective shelter basing). This scheme has serious military drawbacks and does not solve the basic problem, which is the current vulnerability of the Minuteman and Titan force.

A program to deply 100 MX in 1,000 shelters would not be survivable against today's threat, much less the Soviet forces that are likely to be deployed in the mid-1980s.

By the same token, a program to deploy 200 MX missiles in 4,600 shelters has only one significant difference from the 100 in 1,000 plan: it is more expensive (but no more survivable).

The more shelters or holes we build, the more Soviet missiles will be built. They can build missiles as fast as we can build shelters, at about the same cost to both countries.

Any ground-based scheme ultimately would require a ballistic missile defense for survivability. But today, ballistic missile defense technology is not at the stage where it could provide an adequate defense against Soviet missiles.

For the future, we are not yet sure how well ballistic missile defenses will work; what they will cost; how Soviet ballistic missile defenses—which would almost certainly be deployed in response to any U.S. missile defense system—would affect U.S. and allied offensive capabilities; and what would be the political ramifications of altering the ABM (anti-ballistic missile) Treaty.

While it is not the determining factor it should be noted that multiple protective shelter basing has strong environmental opponents who would use every available tactic, and there are many, to delay MX deployment.

We believe there are promising alternative basing modes for MX, and vigorous R & D programs will be initiated on three possibilities.

We are hopeful that one or more of these alternatives will give far greater survivability than multiple protective shelter basing.

We plan to choose among these long-term basing operations as soon as sufficient technical information becomes available, and in any event, no later than 1984.

The MX missile itself will be ready in 1986, well ahead of its long-term basing. Meanwhile, initial deployment in existing ICBM silos is the only way to avoid delaying MX.

We cannot afford to put off MX, a much stronger and more accurate missile than Minuteman, and continue the decade-long pattern of postponement, vacillation and delay.

Early deployment of MX will break the Soviet monopoly on prompt counter-ICBM capabilities.

While not a long-term solution, reconstructing silos (by adding more steel and concrete to help withstand nuclear explosions) would force the Soviets to develop more accurate missiles and might well keep them from achieving a high confidence counter-MX capability until the late 1980s, by which time we will have a better system.

Strategic Defense
Description

We plan to upgrade, in coordination with Canada, the North American air surveillance network. The plan will include some combination of new over-the-horizon backscatter (OTH-B) radars and improved versions of the ground radars that exist today.

We will replace five squadrons of aging F-106 interceptors with new F-15s.

We plan to buy at least six additional Awacs airborne surveillance aircraft for North American air defense to augment ground-based radars in peacetime and to provide surveillance and control interceptors in wartime.

We will continue to pursue an operational antisatellite system.

Research and development on ballistic missile defense will be vigorously pursued.

As discussed under ICBM modernization, we will expand ballistic missile defense R & D for active defense of land-based missiles.

We will develop technologies for space-based missile defense.

An expanded, cost effective, civil defense program will be developed in coordination with the Federal Emergency Management Agency.

We will pursue other related programs and objectives.

Reasons for Program

We have virtually ignored strategic defensive systems for over a decade. As a result, we have large gaps in the North American air defense warning network; our strategic air defense interceptors are obsolete; and our antisatellite and ballistic missile defense programs have lagged behind the Soviets.

The Reagan program ends these years of neglect. We have taken the first steps toward restoring credible strategic defensive forces. In the years ahead, we plan to continue our review of strategic defense to determine what additional steps may be needed.

VULNERABILITY ASSUMES THE SOVIETS WILL STRIKE FIRST[4]

The Carter Administration defined the strategic nuclear options facing America in a cautious and restrained way; yet it proposed what could have been a $100 billion solution of shuttling 200 new MX missiles among 4,600 underground shelters. Last week, the Reagan Administration painted the strategic challenges in far more dire terms, but went on to recommend the much less expensive solution of building 100 MX missiles and simply putting many of them in existing ICBM silos protected by extra concrete.

Behind both responses is the assumption that American land-based intercontinental ballistic missiles are highly vul-

[4] Excerpted from a newspaper article, "Vulnerability Assumes the Soviets Will Strike First," by Leslie H. Gelb, correspondent. *The New York Times,* p. El. O. 4, '81. © 1981 by The New York Times Company. Reprinted by permission.

nerable to a Soviet first strike. It is an assumption, past and present officials agree, that has never received a thorough public airing.

A phalanx of Pentagon planners has told Presidents Carter and Reagan that to assume otherwise would be to risk strategic disaster. An equally solid group of political advisers have argued that it would be political suicide to downplay the threat of a Soviet first strike. . . .

President Reagan and Defense Secretary Caspar W. Weinberger said that any form of the Carter idea to seek safety in a gigantic shell game system would not work. The Soviets, Mr. Weinberger pointed out, could always deploy more nuclear warheads to overwhelm it.

But Mr. Weinberger did not explain how his idea of superhard silos could resist increasingly accurate Soviet warheads, when most Pentagon experts say they cannot. Nor did he elaborate on how his proposed longterm options to be developed—such as ballistic missile defense of the MX—would help. These solutions could not be ready until near the end of the decade, and Mr. Weinberger now says that "the window of vulnerability" will be during 1984–87.

All of the still unanswered questions are likely to prompt Congress to examine the issues that lay behind the Reagan decision. The examination may well focus on the following scenario, which military planners have relied upon to justify MX:

There is a crisis, perhaps a conventional shooting war between the Soviet Union and the United States in the Persian Gulf. Moscow believes that Washington is about to launch a nuclear first strike that could destroy the bulk of Soviet missiles and long-range bombers, so Soviet leaders decide to strike the first blow themselves. They launch about 200 of their biggest missiles, each armed with 10 nuclear warheads, and 95 percent of the 1,000 American Minuteman ICBM's are destroyed. Thus, almost all of America's best weapons for striking back quickly and destroying protected military and command targets in the Soviet Union are gone. The President is now left with an impossible choice: either attack Soviet cities and invite a Soviet response against American cities with deaths in the scores of millions or surrender. Checkmate.

For this scenario to be plausible, however, Soviet leaders would have to assume: 1) the Soviet attack would be virtually flawless; 2) the President would allow the Minutemen to stay in their silos and be destroyed; and 3) the President would regard the attack against Minuteman sites, which could kill instantly somewhere between 5 and 20 million Americans in the vicinity as "limited," not requiring an instant response. There is considerable disagreement among nuclear strategists on whether all of these conditions would ever be met.

The Perfect Attack. If the prospects for a near perfect first strike are not good, leaving, say, as many as 200 or more Minuteman missiles intact and available to strike at Soviet targets, even Washington's hawks agree that Soviet interest in a first strike would fall off sharply. Perfection entails Soviet missiles flying 6,000 miles, releasing warheads with the explosive power of one megaton, or a million tons of TNT, that would land about 500 feet from the target. This is what is required to destroy a missile silo hardened to resist some 2,000 pounds of pressure per square inch.

American intelligence experts agree that Soviet test firings have demonstrated the necessary accuracy. But these firings have been on an East-West axis, while land-based missiles fired at North American targets would have to pass over the North Pole. (Submarine-launched missiles are not considered accurate enough to aim at hardened silos.) Since it normally takes several tests to correct for the effects of gravity, weather and other biases, and because Moscow has not tested over the Pole, some experts contend that Soviet leaders could not have sufficient confidence of a perfect attack. Most authorities insist, however, that information from satellites now allows for mapping of gravity fields and weather, and they point to the successful launching of space platforms aimed at planets millions of miles away as a demonstration of what can be done. But whoever is right now, the necessary accuracy is likely to be available by the end of the decade. Then, satellites will be able to redirect missile trajectories in-flight and guide the warheads precisely to their targets.

In the end, Soviet leaders, not computers and planners, will have to make the decision about the odds for perfection. While most Soviet experts might tell their leaders the capability is there, some almost certainly will point out the great stakes, risks, and uncertainties.

Not Launching United States Missiles. If prepared to make the assumption of perfection, Soviet leaders would also have to assume that the President would not fire the Minutemen before they are destroyed. In about 10 minutes, the President, drawing on information from surveillance satellites and radar warning stations, would probably know with great confidence how many Soviet missiles were in-flight and what their targets were.

Why would Soviet leaders believe the President would not fire the Minutemen? Like the Pentagon planners, they know that if the Minutemen are launched and destroy most of the unfired Soviet land-based missiles, a Soviet first strike would make no sense at all. The plausibility of the scenario rests on the Soviets having hundreds of missiles in reserve that can strike quickly and accurately after they have destroyed almost all comparable American missiles in a first strike. If they, like the United States, are left only with less-accurate missiles suitable for attacking such large targets as cities, neither side wins.

But, say those who take the first-strike scenario seriously, the President might fear an error in his early warning system and decline to launch the Minutemen. They say that a launch-under-attack plan is too risky, and that mistakes have been made before. Others counter that the risks can be minimized by increasing command, communications and early warning capabilities—to give the President more confidence in his information.

Would Soviet leaders bet that the President would be frozen by the prospect of a mistake? Most American intelligence analysts maintain that Soviet leaders themselves rely on a launch-under-attack doctrine.

Armageddon or Surrender. Despite the millions of casualties that a strike on United States missile silos would cause, Soviet leaders would have to assume that the President would regard this as a limited attack. They would have to believe that the President would say something like the following to himself: "I have practically no Minutemen left to strike at hardened Soviet military targets. I can use my remaining bombers and submarine-launched missiles only against Soviet cities. But even if I destroy Soviet urban centers, Moscow will retaliate against American cities, and the result will be tens of millions dead on both sides. Armageddon. Better to surrender."

What grounds would Soviet leaders have to assume that with so many Americans killed, more than in all wars the United States has fought put together, the conflict would be thought of as limited? Why wouldn't they assume that the President would at least seek to equalize the dead and call it a draw by retaliating against "soft" military targets like airfields and tank factories near cities to equalize the destruction?

Those who believe in the first Soviet strike scenario usually argue that while all the criticisms may be sound, they overlook the broader political context. The possibility that America might be vulnerable to attack gives Moscow great confidence and leaves Washington feeling weak, the believers say. Consequently, Soviet leaders might press toward a crisis with greater confidence, as Washington did at the time of the showdown over Soviet missiles in Cuba in 1962, and that the President might be forced to make concessions out of weakness. Moreover, they argue, the United States is rich and powerful enough so that it can afford insurance against these possibilities—be it the MX missile system or whatever. Further, they maintain, providing such insurance would reassure America's allies.

The first-strike scenario has been debated behind-the-scenes among experts for many years, although few have altered their views, one way or the other. But on those rare occasions when subjective judgments are set aside, most authorities agree on the following:

First, it is mainly a debate about the psychology of power, more than about the likelihood of an actual attack. Because of the strategic balance, which side would act with confidence and which with fear—these are the key issues underlying the debate.

Second, even after the most successful imaginable Soviet attack, Washington would still have about 3,500 nuclear warheads at its disposal. As of now, the Soviet Union has some 7,000 and the United States about 9,000, and both stockpiles are growing.

Third, even if United States ICBM's are all that vulnerable, there are no quick fixes to the vulnerability. Solutions that might work could take at least five or six years.

Fourth, if the problem is real, it is extremely difficult for planners to work out a solution that does not involve strategic arms control. Without negotiated limits, each side always will be able to improve and increase its arsenal.

Mr. Reagan now is in a box. He continues to assert that there is a real and present danger to the ICBM's, yet his new programs do nothing to alleviate that danger. His interim solution—hardening silos—is a tacit admission that there are no short-term answers. He apparently isn't sure whether there are long-term answers either.

AT 'A MINIMUM $200 MILLION A BIRD,' B–1 BOMBER DEBATE BEGINS[5]

The Administration's plan for upgrading the United States's nuclear arsenal came under heavy attack last week.

[5] Excerpted from a newspaper article "At 'a Minimum $200 Million a Bird,' B-1 Bomber Debate Begins," interviews conducted by Richard Halloran, Pentagon correspondent, with Rep. William L. Dickinson (R-Ala.) and Sen. Gary Hart (D.-Colo.). *The New York Times.* E5. O. 11, '81. Copyright © 1981 by The New York Times Company. Reprinted by permission.

Secretary of Defense Caspar W. Weinberger testified that the $180.3 billion program would create a "stable and secure" deterrent, but Capitol Hill wasn't so sure. Some members of Congress set their sights on the proposal to install new MX missiles in superhardened Titan silos. Others claimed that a resurrected B-1 would be a bomber without a future.

A leading proponent of the B-1 is William L. Dickinson of Alabama, senior Republican on the House Armed Services Committee. An influential opponent is Gary Hart, Democrat of Colorado and a member of the Senate Armed Services Committee. They were interviewed separately by Richard Halloran, The New York Times's Pentagon correspondent. Mr. Halloran first asked each why he approved or disapproved of the President's proposal.

William L. Dickinson

Mr. Dickinson. What has to be weighed in the balance is this: Do we go forward with the B-1 or with the advanced technology bomber, so-called Stealth, or with both? We need both, it seems to me.

The earliest delivery date of the Stealth would be 1988, 1989, 1990. Something in that time frame—if all goes well. It might in fact be 1991, 1992, 1993—we don't know for sure. It is, after all, still in the research and development stage. So, and this is what I urged on the President, just don't drop the bird in the hand for two in the bush. Particularly when they say you can't see the two in the bush.

What the President has proposed is a sensible approach. We have a known technology. We have built four B-1 bombers; we have flown four. We know the state of the art, and the technology is at hand—the tools, dies, rigs, whatever—so we know what we could do with that. We've also flown it against radar and we have a very high degree of confidence in its ability to penetrate.

If I had any heartburn at all, it has to do with the cost of the program. The projected cost of the original plane started off at something like $50 million a plane, went to $60 million and then to $70 million. When the project was canceled by President Carter, we were looking at real cost of somewhere around $90 million a plane. Now they've thrown a $20 billion to $30 billion program at us. You divide that out it comes out to a minimum of $200 million a bird.

But that's not the fault of the weapons system itself. If Carter hadn't canceled it, we would have the B-1 in production already or be very close to it. It would have a substantial capability but at about half of what we're proposing to spend now.

Question. In his testimony before your committee and before the Senate committee as well, Defense Secretary Weinberger talked about the need to fill the gap between the retirement of the B-52 and the addition of the Stealth to the Air Force arsenal, in maybe another seven or eight years. Why do you think we need to cover that period with the B-1? Why can't we just extend the life of the B-52 a few more years?

A. In the final analysis, it comes back to credibility and what is sufficient for deterrence. And now even if you enhance the capability of the B-52 sufficiently to have a penetration capability, the cost is tremendous. And you still have a 30-year-old-bird. So this is part of the equation; I don't think it's ever discussed: if you don't build a B-1, what are you going to do?

So you can't ignore that fact, the cost of making do with the B-52, when you're considering the need for the B-1. You have to consider the window of vulnerability—are you closing the window or just pulling a shade down on it?

Q. Mr. Weinberger says that we're going to have the first B-1's in 1986. Given the track record of defense contractors, do you think they can deliver on time?

A. Well, I'm shaking my head in befuddlement. That's a negative reply, the reason being that when we were discussing, initially, about two years ago, with the president of Rockwell, how soon could he rev up and go forward if this decision to cancel were changed—and he said it would take less than four years. About four years to rev up from where they were then.

But there's been a lot of water over the dam since then. Certainly the cost has escalated. Even with a scaled-down capability—that is, not sweeping the wings as far, or taking all that mechanism out of the center of the thing and generally lightening the plane. Two years ago, we were told that if you reduced the air intakes, if you do away with some other things that were required for supersonic flight, then Rockwell could build the new version cheaper than the proposed cost of the original version. But the cost hasn't been scaled down. It's escalated, for whatever reason, dramatically.

Q. Let me just ask a somewhat philosophical question. Why do we need any new manned strategic bomber, the B-1 or the Stealth? Can't missiles do the job?

A. If you're thinking only in the strategic mode, you might be right. But you can't drop a nuke on everybody that you're going to fight. You're got to have some in-hand capability in conventional weaponry.

The B-52's been a very formidable weapon. President Johnson was very short-sighted and wrong in first committing them in Southeast Asia, knowing they were out of production, and putting them at risk, which they were, of being shot down. And then on such a limited basis that they couldn't even hit the most valuable targets. We were putting them in a very high-risk situation and risking them on low-value targets. And that was dumb. Of course, the whole damn thing was dumb. He should never have got us in there if we weren't planning to win.

Anyway, the B-52 has been a very good bird and very dependable and now that they're 30 years old, they're a bit decrepit and their value is becoming increasingly limited as the accuracy of surface-to-air missiles gets better and better. . . .

Also, if we give our enemies a new weapons system to worry about—a B-1 bomber—then this complicates their problems. They want to protect Moscow and their other cities. They believe in having a redundancy of defenses that won't wait. We force them to spend that much more on defense with a new weapon. Then if you come on later with the Stealth, you've given them still more to worry about. They'll be outspending us 5 to 1 just to counter what we're doing. And whatever they spend on defense takes away from what they can spend on offensive weapons.

Gary Hart

Mr. Hart. I'm opposed to (the proposal), as I was when the issue arose four years ago, for primarily the same reasons. There are not enough defense dollars to buy both the B-1 and the Stealth, and the air-launched cruise missile program. The cruise missile program, moreover, offers a more than sufficient bridge between the availability of the current manned bomber force—the B-52's—and what I think ought to be the next manned bomber, the Stealth. Finally, the cost of the B-1 program will drain necessary funds away from both our strategic forces and from conventional force modernization.

Question. Defense officials insist that we need a new bomber sandwiched in between the retirement of the B-52 and the introduction of the Stealth. What do you think?

A. I think that particular window of vulnerability is a narrow one. First of all there's been a dispute over the useful life of the B-52. If given a cruise missile carrier role, it certainly has a longer useful life than if it were merely a manned penetrating bomber. And we are in the process of converting the B-52H to that role and we will have those available starting next year.

If we put a lot of the money that the Administration proposes for the B-1 program into the Stealth program, accelerated it, we would shrink the window from the other side. And the cruise missile program could extend the life and effective use of the B-52 from this end.

Q. Estimates of the cost of the B-1 program range between $20 billion and $30 billion. Do those figures seem reasonable to you?

A. I've seen estimates ranging anywhere from $15 billion to $50 billion. I think $20 billion to $30 billion is on the low side. The problem in this whole arena is how much of the support equipment gets loaded into the total program cost.

People who want to project the lowest possible cost for a system don't put those things in; they just give you the figure for that system itself in its total buy, but none of the tankers, none of the operations and maintenance or support facilities. If you add all it would take to get this airplane in the air and keep it running, then you're reaching to a much higher level.

Q. If we build the advanced version of the B-1, do we really need Stealth? Why can't we load the B-1 with some of the Stealth technology and delay introduction of Stealth itself until, say, the mid or the late '90s?

A. You can't. We don't have the Stealth technology yet so you can't build it into the B-1 bomber. That's the Achilles heel of the B-1 bomber. It is an obsolete technology, given both existing and projected Soviet defensive capabilities. It will be obsolete by the time it's deployed.

Stealth is a breakthrough. It would leapfrog technology instead of challenging technology. What the B-1 bomber does is accept a certain given of Soviet technology and say, 'We're going to go right at it and try to defeat it.' And that's its fatal flaw. Stealth says, 'We know what that technology is going to be and we're going to leapfrog it by sophisticated counter-technology.'

B-1 would offer no particular threat or challenge to the Soviets; Stealth makes obsolete what they have and what they will have, and forces them into a defensive mode which requires an enormous capital investment.

Q. But supposing the United States does leapfrog over B-1 and proceed directly with development of Stealth. Won't the Russians have time to catch up with the defensive technology?

A. Well, that might be the case if technology can be forced; that is to say, they know a bomber is coming which is going to have an almost nonexistent radar profile, and therefore all they've got to do is invent a way to find it. We have found out that's not as easy as it may sound. Laymen, such as myself, tend to think that scientists can do anything. Quite often they can't.

You could have argued 10 or 15 or 20 years ago, 'Let's not build the Trident because by the time it's built there will be strategic antisubmarine warfare capability.' Well, there isn't. Some things you just can't force. I don't think by the late '80s, even if the Soviets know we're coming with a bomber that's different and hard to find, that they'll find out a way to find it.

Q. *In the longterm, are we really going to need a manned bomber at all? Why not build a cheap air-launched cruise missile carrier and let it go at that?*

A. We probably will need a manned bomber for two reasons: One, it's recallable. If bombers are sent out, and you later discover that mistakes were made or your radar turned out to be wrong, you've got time to call them back. It's the only human system of all the strategic systems.

The second point is that part of strategic survivability and deterrence is creating a situation where your opponent cannot target only one or two systems. That's the value of the so-called triad. It is not merely a strategic concept, created to satisfy the many armed services we have. Rather, it creates a kind of jujitsu puzzle for the Soviets. They don't have to throw just the submarine or just a land-based system; they've got to figure out a way to throw three of them.

And when they figure one system out, then you're ahead of them on the other. Then they've got to race over there and try to figure out how to defeat that one. And while they're focused on that, then you can do the other system. To the layman, I think it sounds a little more esoteric than it really is. It's just a practical application of not concentrating your defenses in one arena.

Q. *Does the manned strategic bomber have a role in conventional war?*

A. Yes, in perhaps a war in Europe or in the Persian Gulf region, where the super powers are in confrontation. There are all kinds of instant histories of the role of the bomber in Vietnam, for example, a third world scenario as to whether it did any good or not. If you believe the war was ended by the bombings of North Vietnam, then the answer to your question is 'yes.' If you believe that, by and large, the Vietnamese figured out a way to survive in spite of the carpet bombings, then your answer is 'no.'

I would put it this way: I don't think the manned bomber is the most effective weapon in small third world wars. And those are the ones I think we'll face in the '80s and '90s.

U.S. PROGRAM FOR PEACE AND ARMS CONTROL[6]

. . . I want to speak today to this audience, and the people of the world, about America's program for peace and the coming negotiations which begin November 30th in Geneva, Switzerland. Specifically, I want to present our program for preserving peace in Europe and our wider program for arms control.

Preserving Peace

Twice in my lifetime I have seen the peoples of Europe plunged into the tragedy of war. Twice in my lifetime Europe has suffered destruction and military occupation in wars that statesmen proved powerless to prevent, soldiers unable to contain, and ordinary citizens unable to escape. And twice in my lifetime, young Americans have bled their lives into the soil of those battlefields—not to enrich or enlarge our domain but to restore the peace and independence of our friends and allies.

All of us who lived through those troubled times share a common resolve that they must never come again. And most of us share a common appreciation of the Atlantic alliance that has made a peaceful, free, and prosperous Western Europe in the postwar era possible.

But today a new generation is emerging on both sides of the Atlantic. Its members were not present at the creation of the North Atlantic alliance. Many of them do not fully un-

[6] Excerpts of an address by Ronald Reagan, President of the United States, before the National Press Club, Washington, D.C. November 18, 1981. *Department of State Bulletin.* 81:10–13. D. '81.

derstand its roots in defending freedom and rebuilding a war-torn continent. Some young people question why we need weapons—particularly nuclear weapons—to deter war and to assure peaceful development. They fear that the accumulation of weapons itself may lead to conflagration. Some even propose unilateral disarmament.

I understand their concerns. Their questions deserve to be answered. But we have an obligation to answer their questions on the basis of judgment and reason and experience. Our policies have resulted in the longest European peace in this century. Would not a rash departure from these policies, as some now suggest, endanger that peace? From its founding, the Atlantic alliance has preserved the peace through unity, deterrence, and dialogue.

First, we and our allies have stood united by the firm commitment that an attack upon any one of us would be considered an attack upon us all;

Second, we and our allies have deterred aggression by maintaining forces strong enough to insure that any aggressor would lose more from an attack than he could possibly gain; and

Third, we and our allies have engaged the Soviets in a dialogue about mutual restraint and arms limitations, hoping to reduce the risk of war and the burden of armaments and to lower the barriers that divide East from West.

These three elements of our policy have preserved the peace in Europe for more than a third of a century. They can preserve it for generations to come, so long as we pursue them with sufficient will and vigor.

Today, I wish to reaffirm America's commitment to the Atlantic alliance and our resolve to sustain the peace. And from my conversations with allied leaders, I know that they also remain true to this tried and proven course. NATO's policy of peace is based on restraint and balance. No NATO weapons, conventional or nuclear, will ever be used in Europe except in response to attack. NATO's defense plans have been responsible and restrained. The allies remain strong, united, and resolute. But the momentum of the continuing Soviet military buildup threatens both the conventional and the nuclear balance. Consider the facts over the past decade:

—The United States reduced the size of its armed forces and decreased its military spending. The Soviets steadily increased the number of men under arms. They now number more than double those of the United States. Over the same period the Soviets expanded their real military spending by about one-third.

—The Soviet Union increased its inventory of tanks to some 50,000 compared to our 11,000. Historically a landpower, they transformed their navy from a coastal defense force to an open ocean fleet, while the United States, a seapower with transoceanic alliances, cut its fleet in half.

—During a period when NATO deployed no new intermediate-range nuclear missiles and actually withdrew 1,000 nuclear warheads, the Soviet Union deployed more than 750 nuclear warheads on the new SS-20 missiles alone.

Our response to this relentless buildup of Soviet military power has been restrained but firm. We have made decisions to strengthen all three legs of the strategic triad—sea-, land-, and air-based. We have proposed a defense program in the United States for the next 5 years which will remedy the neglect of the past decade and restore the eroding balance on which our security depends.

I would like to discuss more specifically the growing threat to Western Europe which is posed by the continuing deployment of certain Soviet intermediate-range nuclear missiles. The Soviet Union has three different types of such missile systems—the SS-20, the SS-4, and the SS-5—all with a range capable of reaching virtually all of Western Europe. There are other Soviet weapons systems which also represent a major threat. The only answer to these systems is a comparable threat to Soviet targets. In other words, a deterrent preventing the use of these Soviet weapons by the counterthreat of a like response against their own territory.

At present, however, there is no equivalent deterrent to these Soviet intermediate missiles. And the Soviets continue to add one new SS-20 a week. To counter this, the allies agreed in 1979, as part of a two-track decision, to deploy as a deterrent land-based cruise missiles and Pershing II missiles capable of reaching targets in the Soviet Union. These missiles are to be deployed in several countries of Western Europe.

This relatively limited force in no way serves as a substitute for the much larger strategic umbrella spread over our NATO allies. Rather, it provides a vital link between conventional, shorter range nuclear forces in Europe and intercontinental forces in the United States. Deployment of these systems will demonstrate to the Soviet Union that this link cannot be broken.

Deterring war depends on the perceived ability of our forces to perform effectively. The more effective our forces are, the less likely it is that we'll have to use them. So, we and our allies are proceeding to modernize NATO's nuclear forces of intermediate range to meet increased Soviet deployments of nuclear systems threatening Western Europe.

Arms Control Negotiations

Let me turn now to our hopes for arms control negotiations. There is a tendency to make this entire subject overly complex. I want to be clear and concise. . . . The United States proposes the mutual reduction of conventional, intermediate-range nuclear and strategic forces. Specifically, I have proposed a four-point agenda to achieve this objective in my letter to President Brezhnev.

The first, and most important, point concerns the Geneva negotiations. As part of the 1979 two-track decision, NATO made a commitment to seek arms control negotiations with the Soviet Union on intermediate-range nuclear forces. The United States has been preparing for these negotiations through close consultation with our NATO partners. We are now ready to set forth our proposal. I have informed President Brezhnev that when our delegation travels to the negotiations on intermediate-range land-based nuclear missiles in Geneva on the 30th of this month, my representatives will present the following proposal: The United States is prepared to cancel its deployment of Pershing II and ground-launch cruise missiles if the Soviets will dismantle their SS-20, SS-4, and SS-5 missiles. This would be an historic step. With Soviet agreement, we could together substantially reduce the dread threat of nuclear war which hangs over the people of Europe. This, like the first footstep on the moon, would be a giant step for mankind.

We intend to negotiate in good faith and go to Geneva willing to listen to and consider the proposals of our Soviet counterparts. But let me call to your attention the background against which our proposal is made. During the past 6 years, while the United States deployed no new intermediate-range missiles and withdrew 1,000 nuclear warheads from Europe, the Soviet Union deployed 750 warheads on mobile, accurate ballistic missiles. They now have 1,100 warheads on the SS-20, SS-4, and SS-5 missiles, and the United States has no comparable missiles. Indeed, the United States dismantled the last such missile in Europe over 15 years ago.

As we look to the future of the negotiations, it is also important to address certain Soviet claims which, left unrefuted, could become critical barriers to real progress in arms control. The Soviets assert that a balance of intermediate-range nuclear forces already exists. That assertion is wrong. By any objective measure, . . . the Soviet Union has an overwhelming advantage, on the order of six to one.

Soviet spokesmen have suggested that moving their SS-20s beyond the Ural Mountains will remove the threat to Europe. . . . The SS-20s, even if deployed behind the Urals, will have a range that places almost all of Western Europe, the great cities, Rome, Athens, Paris, London, Brussels, Amsterdam, Berlin, and so many more; all of Scandinavia; all of the Middle East; all of northern Africa—all within range of these missiles, which incidentally are mobile and can be moved on short notice.

The second proposal I've made to President Brezhnev concerns strategic weapons. The United States proposes to open negotiations on strategic arms as soon as possible next year. I have instructed Secretary Haig to discuss the timing of such meetings with Soviet representatives.

Substance, however, is far more important than timing. As our proposal for the Geneva talks this month illustrates, we can make proposals for genuinely serious reductions but only if we take the time to prepare carefully. The United States has been preparing carefully for resumption of strategic arms negotiations because we do not want a repetition of past disappointments. We don't want an arms control process that sends hopes soaring only to end in dashed expectations.

I have informed President Brezhnev that we will seek to negotiate substantial reductions in nuclear arms which would result in levels that are equal and verifiable. Our approach to verification will be to emphasize openness and creativity— rather than the secrecy and suspicion which have undermined confidence in arms control in the past.

While we can hope to benefit from work done over the past decade in strategic arms negotiations, let us agree to do more than simply begin where these previous efforts left off. We can and should attempt major qualitative and quantitative progress. Only such progress can fulfill the hopes of our own people and the rest of the world. And let us see how far we can go in achieving truly substantial reductions in our strategic arsenals. To symbolize this fundamental change in direction, we will call these negotiations START—Strategic Arms Reduction Talks.

The third proposal I have made to the Soviet Union is that we act to achieve equality at lower levels of conventional forces in Europe. The defense needs of the Soviet Union hardly call for maintaining more combat divisions in East Germany today than were in the whole Allied invasion force that landed in Normandy on D-day. The Soviet Union could make no more convincing contribution to peace in Europe— and in the world—than by agreeing to reduce its conventional forces significantly and constrain the potential for sudden aggression.

Finally, I have pointed out to President Brezhnev that to maintain peace, we must reduce the risks of surprise attack and the chance of war arising out of uncertainty or miscalculation. I am renewing our proposal for a conference to develop effective measures that would reduce these dangers. At the current Madrid meeting of the Conference on Security and Cooperation in Europe, we are laying the foundation for a Western-proposed conference on disarmament in Europe. This conference would discuss new measures to enhance stability and security in Europe. Agreement on this conference is within reach. I urge the Soviet Union to join us and many other nations who are ready to launch this important enterprise.

All of these proposals are based on the same fair-minded principles: substantial, militarily significant reduction in forces; equal ceilings for similar types of forces; and adequate provisions for verification. My Administration, our country, and I are committed to achieving arms reduction agreements based on these principles. Today, I have outlined the kinds of bold, equitable proposals which the world expects of us. But we cannot reduce arms unilaterally. Success can only come if the Soviet Union will share our commitment; if it will demonstrate that its often-repeated professions of concern for peace will be matched by positive action.

U.S. Concept of Peace

Preservation of peace in Europe and the pursuit of arms reduction talks are of fundamental importance. But we must also help to bring peace and security to regions now torn by conflict, external intervention, and war.

The American concept of peace goes well beyond the absence of war. We foresee a flowering of economic growth and individual liberty in a world at peace. At the economic summit conference in Cancun, I met with the leaders of 21 nations and sketched out our approach to global economic growth. We want to eliminate the barriers to trade and investment which hinder these critical incentives to growth. And we're working to develop new programs to help the poorest nations achieve self-sustaining growth.

KEY INTERMEDIATE-RANGE LAND-BASED MISSILES

Soviet					US			
Type	Warheads per Missile	Number of Launchers Deployed	Total Warheads on Launchers	Range (km)	Total Warheads on Launchers	Number of Launchers Deployed	Warheads per Missile	Type
SS–20	3	250	750	4,400 to 5,000				—
SS–5	1	35	35	4,100				—
—				2,500	0 (464 planned)	0 (116 launchers, 4 missiles per launcher planned)	1	Ground-launched cruise missile
SS–4	1	315	315	1,900				—
—		—		1,800	0 (108 planned)	0 (108 planned)	1	Pershing II
Total		600	1,100	0	0 (572 planned)	0 (224 planned)		**Total**

And terms like "peace" and "security," we have to say, have little meaning for the oppressed and the destitute. They also mean little to the individual whose state has stripped him of human freedom and dignity. Wherever there is oppression, we must strive for the peace and security of individuals as well as states. We must recognize that progress in the pursuit of liberty is a necessary complement to military security. Nowhere has this fundamental truth been more boldly and clearly stated than in the Helsinki accords of 1975. These accords have not yet been translated into living reality.

Today, I have announced an agenda that can help to achieve peace, security, and freedom across the globe. In particular, I have made an important offer to forego entirely deployment of new American missiles in Europe if the Soviet Union is prepared to respond on an equal footing.

There is no reason why people in any part of the world should have to live in permanent fear of war or its specter. I believe the time has come for all nations to act in a responsible spirit that doesn't threaten other states. I believe the time is right to move forward on arms control and the resolution of critical regional disputes at the conference table. Nothing will have a higher priority for me and for the American people over the coming months and years.

Addressing the United Nations 20 years ago, another American President described the goal we still pursue today. He said, "If we all can persevere, if we can . . . look beyond our own shores and ambitions, then surely the age will dawn in which the strong are just and the weak secure and the peace preserved." He didn't live to see that goal achieved.

I invite all nations to join with America today in the quest for such a world.   •

III. U.S. CONVENTIONAL FORCES

EDITOR'S INTRODUCTION

Strategic weapons are only one aspect of the U.S.–Soviet military rivalry. Conventional (non-nuclear) forces are equally important in maintaining balances in Central Europe and East Asia, and in creating a U.S. military presence in the Middle East. These conventional forces, which account for about 90% of U.S. defense spending, play a more important part than nuclear weapons in discussions of defense needs and budgets.

In the first article in this section, William W. Kaufmann of the Brookings Institution analyzes the Carter and Reagan 5-year plans for U.S. conventional forces. The staff of *Business Week* examines the Reagan administration's plans to expand the U.S. Navy, and Admiral Stansfield Turner, former CIA Director, criticizes the U.S. Navy's emphasis on large aircraft carriers. He makes a case for smaller and more numerous flat-tops.

Most military analysts believe that the Persian Gulf is one of the most volatile areas of the world, and the Carter administration drew up plans in January 1980 for a "Rapid Deployment Force" for possible intervention to protect U.S. interests in the region. The fourth article in this section, a speech by Carter's Secretary of Defense Harold Brown, outlines the U.S. strategy to protect the Persian Gulf. And in the fifth article, David D. Newsom, Carter's Undersecretary of State, registers his criticisms of both the style and the substance of the "Carter Doctrine" in an article in *Foreign Policy* magazine.

Another important consideration with respect to U.S. conventional forces is the design of weapons. In the last two articles in this section George C. Wilson asks, "Are our weapons too complex?" William J. Perry, interviewed by Wilson, insists that they are not: "Not if you compare them to the Russians'."

NONNUCLEAR PROBLEMS AND PROGRAMS[1]

A basic theme of the [Carter] five-year program has been that the problems of U.S. and allied conventional forces are much more serious than those of the nuclear forces and are more costly to overcome. Except for the Navy, which continued to shrink during the Carter presidency (because of small shipbuilding programs in the Nixon and Ford years), the conventional forces themselves are not yet seen as requiring any major growth, especially given the real difficulty of manning existing capabilities. The rationale behind the five-year plan has been that these forces are large enough to deal with any two nonnuclear contingencies that might arise, including even a large-scale attack by the Warsaw Pact on Central Europe. Whether the conventional forces could respond to the contingencies in a timely fashion, fight with full effectiveness, and sustain themselves in combat at least as long as potential enemies has been, however, considered much less certain, particularly when the Soviet Union ... is credited with being able to attack areas contiguous to it on very short notice.

The problems of effectiveness are judged to have arisen primarily from the shortage of funds for the spare parts, major overhauls, and experienced military personnel required to help keep operational equipment in good working order. Because operation and maintenance activities are alleged to have been shortchanged in the past and because military pay has been eroded by inflation, key enlisted personnel have been leaving the services for more lucrative civilian work, and substantial percentages of U.S. ships, aircraft, and tracked vehicles have not been considered capable of performing their assigned missions. Flying hours and steaming

[1] Excerpt from the chapter entitled "The Defense Budget," by William W. Kaufmann, professor at the Massachusetts Institute of Technology, in the book *Setting National Priorities: The 1982 Budget.* Joseph A. Pechman, ed. The Brookings Institution, 1981. pp. 150–7. Copyright © 1981 by The Brookings Institution. Reprinted by permission.

days have fallen, not only because of maintenance and over-haul problems, but also because of the rising cost of petro-leum products. Combat effectiveness allegedly has fallen commensurately.

From the standpoint of the five-year defense program, at least in its current form, the quickest and cheapest way to re-store combat effectiveness is not to add more maintenance-prone force structure but to repair and exploit fully the capa-bility of those forces already in existence. In line with this philosophy, military pay in general was increased by 11.7 percent in fiscal 1981, and the Reagan administration plans to raise the total by $420 million in 1981 and by nearly $1.9 bil-lion in 1982. In addition, special efforts are being made to re-tain military personnel critical to matériel readiness. Opera-tion and maintenance accounts are being funded at levels that will reduce overhaul backlogs to appropriate peacetime levels (usually considered to be 10 to 15 percent of the equip-ment), restore inventories of spare parts to the point at which deliveries are prompt and cannibalization of other systems is abandoned, and increase operating rates for ships, aircraft, and ground combat vehicles. As a consequence, operation and maintenance has grown from $46.6 billion in fiscal 1980 to $64.1 billion in fiscal 1982. The real increase over the two-year period amounts to more than 15 percent. This "full funding" of the accounts will presumably be maintained over the period of the five-year defense program.

What constitutes responsiveness to a contingency depends on the nature of the threat and the theater being threatened. For three years the Carter administration, in focusing almost exclusively on the European theater, postulated a threat to Germany from the Warsaw Pact that would be nearly ninety divisions in size and would materialize in several weeks. Since the European allies were not expected to furnish more than a few major reinforcements to the units already on the line, this meant that the United States would have to bear the main burden of stabilizing the central front. Yet U.S. reinforce-ments, with the airlift then on hand or likely to become avail-able in the foreseeable future, would not arrive early enough to prevent a large, fast-moving Warsaw Pact attack from rupturing the allied line.

To extract additional contributions from the European members of NATO and to lay the groundwork for a much speedier deployment of American reinforcements, the United States once again (as it had several times before) launched an elaborate long-term defense plan for the Alliance. At its center has been a U.S. program to store full sets of army division equipment (known as POMCUS) and large war reserve stocks in Germany. These would permit troops to be flown rapidly to Germany, where they would draw the stored equipment and move to the front before an attack.

Whether such a scheme could be made to work on a large scale, or could even be fully tested, has been questioned. Nonetheless, four division sets have already been pre-positioned in Germany, and the Carter program calls for adding two more. At the same time, preparations are being made to deploy as many as forty-two squadrons of fighter-attack aircraft to Europe within ten days. Although the movement of so many ground and air units would put a heavy strain on the KC-135 tanker force—and do so at a time when the Strategic Air Command would need heavy tanker support also—the Carter 1982 budget does not call for the acquisition of any new KC-10 tanker aircraft beyond the twelve already funded through the fiscal 1981 budget. Now, however, the Reagan administration requests $500 million for eight additional KC-10s and about $220 million to begin replacing the engines in the old KC-135 tanker fleet. The newer tankers would be available to support deployments to another theater, as well as Europe, provided that such deployment occurred well before or after the European contingency.

Potential trouble in the area of the Persian Gulf became a source of major concern to the Department of Defense even before the oil embargo of 1973. However, the threat remained difficult to define for planning purposes, and did not begin to attract funding and forces until after the seizure of the American hostages in Iran and the Soviet invasion of Afghanistan. The headquarters for a Rapid Deployment

Force was put together in the wake of these events, with a deployment to the Persian Gulf as its first mission. Soon thereafter, two attack carrier battle groups drawn from the Sixth Fleet (in the Mediterranean) and the Seventh Fleet (in the Western Pacific) went on patrol in the Arabian Sea. Since then, the carrier battle groups have become a more or less permanent fixture in the area, and a reinforced Marine Corps battalion aboard amphibious ships has also been deployed to the Arabian Sea.

Despite these changes, the Carter administration took the position that the capabilities already incorporated in the force structure for a minor contingency (say three or four divisions and five or six fighter wings) were sufficient to cope with an emergency in the gulf. The problems raised by this particular set of dangers were seen to be of a different order than would be solved by additional combat force structure. These problems arose from such difficulties as the increased probability of short-warning attacks by Soviet land forces in the vicinity of the theater; the distance from the United States to the Persian Gulf, computed for airlift at about 9,500 nautical miles; the lack of any en route or forward bases under U.S. control nearer than Diego Garcia in the Indian Ocean, or of war reserve stocks and communications close by; and finally, the difficulties of terrain and climate and the acute shortage of potable water in key parts of the theater— so different from the problems of Europe and Northeast Asia.

Not only did the Carter administration direct its main programs for the Persian Gulf both in fiscal 1981 and in the current five-year defense program toward the solution of these problems; the Reagan administration seems to have accepted these solutions also. The new naval and Marine Corps forward deployments in the vicinity of the gulf have apparently been considered sufficient for presence and to guard against surprise attacks from the north. Hence the key short-term measures have emphasized the acquisition of base rights (however tenuous) in Kenya, Somalia, Egypt, and Oman, and the improvement of ports and bases in these countries and expansion of the base at Diego Garcia in the Indian Ocean;

the earmarking, training, and equipment of general purpose forces for operations in the theater; and the improvement of the U.S. capability for rapidly reinforcing the deployed forces. Particularly noteworthy has been the acquisition of seven commercial cargo ships that are now stationed in the Indian Ocean with the equipment and initial supplies for a full Marine Corps brigade force of 12,000 men. In the event of a crisis and warning of an impending attack, they will permit the troops of the brigade to be flown to the theater in a few days and to join the equipment. In the short run, perhaps an additional light brigade with its equipment could be airlifted to the area within a week, and as much as a division could be brought in by fast sealift ships within thirty to forty days.

For the longer term, the Carter defense program, as it now stands, stresses the acquisition of 12 specially designed maritime pre-positioning ships for the forward deployment of additional equipment and supplies, up to 130 new CX long-range airlift aircraft to supplement the current fleet of C-5s and lengthened C-141s, and the buildup of stocks of war reserve matériel and combat consumables. In addition, the Army is beginning to experiment (presently at modest cost) with the concept of a now light infantry division that would be much more easily airlifted than current units—which are not tailored to existing aircraft—but would have the firepower and mobility to deal with even the heaviest of the Soviet tank divisions.

All these preparations, both short term and longer run, . . . will presumably make the Rapid Deployment Force an all-purpose, minor-contingency force, just as the preparations for Europe are alleged to provide the United States with a flexible major-contingency capability—able to go anywhere anytime. The greater likelihood, however, is that the country will end up with forces trained for and able to deploy to Europe and the Persian Gulf but not particularly adaptable to or available for deployment and combat in other parts of the world.

It was the hope in the early 1960s that a strategic economy of force could be achieved by minimizing overseas deployments and concentrating most U.S. ground and tactical air forces in the continental United States. With the support of selected stocks pre-positioned overseas, fast deployment logistic ships, and airlift, these forces would then be able to move from this central location and respond to contingencies wherever they might occur.

Whether this degree of flexibility has ever been realistically attainable during the past twenty years is open to question. But successive administrations have, for all practical purposes, endorsed the concept at the same time that they have withheld from the forces (particularly the ground forces) the wherewithal to implement the strategy. What were considered the necessary amount and balance of overseas pre-positioning, logistic ships, and airlift have not been acquired. Deployed units (if not numbers of people) have been increased rather than decreased in Europe, and the attempt to withdraw forces from Korea has been abandoned. The renewed alarm about a surprise conventional attack in Europe has had the effect of orienting the majority of the general purpose forces to the central region of NATO. Perhaps most important of all, the task of training and orienting large and complex organizations for a particular contingency—whether in Europe, Korea, or the Persian Gulf—appears to be so great that it precludes the kind of flexibility and all-purpose conventional capability that was envisaged in the strategic concept of the early 1960s. If indeed that is the case, it suggests that the basis for planning U.S. force size and composition will have to change in the future.

The one branch of the U.S. military that can be said to have preserved a large measure of flexibility is the Navy. As it demonstrated by its deployments in the Indian Ocean, it can with a small number of key overseas bases shift its capital ships from one ocean to another without elaborate changes in training, equipment, and logistics. It is evident, however, that the shift did not occur without a certain amount of pain. The Navy, like the other services, lacks the personnel to man and maintain fully the equipment it already has. What is more, the total operating force of general purpose ships (active, reserve, and auxiliary) will consist of only 526 ships in fiscal 1982, whereas the Carter administration had foreseen the need by 1990 for about 550 ships to execute its strategy of long-range blockade, convoy, and power projection. This led to a fourth Carter five-year shipbuilding program of 80 new ships over the period of the five-year program. Such a program, together with the 79 ships previously authorized but not yet delivered, was expected to enable the Navy to reach the goal of 550 ships and even stabilize the force at close to that level through the 1980s, provided that older ships were not phased out more rapidly than is now planned.

The Reagan amendments add to this program in several ways. First, they increase the fiscal 1982 shipbuilding program from fourteen to eighteen ships (about the same as planned by the Carter administration a year ago in a previous five-year shipbuilding program) by adding an AEGIS-equipped air defense cruiser (CG-47), two frigates (FFG-7s), and one nuclear attack submarine (SSN-688) at a cost of over $2 billion. Second, they reactivate two battleships, the *New Jersey* and the *Iowa,* and one aircraft carrier, the *Oriskany,* at a cost of more than $1 billion by fiscal 1983. Third, they request long-lead items for a new amphibious ship (LSD-41) and a new nuclear attack carrier (CVN-72) at a cost of about $700 million. Full funding for these two ships will be requested in fiscal 1983. Presumably the older and less capable ships being reactivated not only will respond "perceptually" to the appearance of the new Soviet *Kirov*-class strike cruisers; they will also provide the nucleus for fifteen battle groups until such time as the Navy again can reach its traditional peacetime goal of fifteen modern, large-deck carriers. Achieving that goal will take quite a few years and many people and dollars.

In the Carter fiscal 1982 budget, funding for the general purpose forces would amount to $74.4 billion (compared to $14.5 billion for the strategic forces). This total does not include more than $3.4 billion for airlift and sealift or $10.3 billion for the National Guard and Reserve forces, even though both programs contain what are primarily general purpose forces. At least 75 percent of the defense budget now goes to these forces and their support. The Reagan amendments actually increase this percentage by adding more than $17 billion to the three programs, with $15.1 billion for the general purpose forces alone.

BUILDING A NAVY TO RULE THE SEAS AGAIN[2]

Defense Secretary Caspar W. Weinberger leaves no doubt about where he stands on the Navy. "We have permitted our naval capability to deteriorate, and now we must restore it," he says. "American commerce and industry and the sinews of the Western alliance depend on our ability to control the seas. We must have naval superiority."

Outnumbered and increasingly challenged by Soviet naval and air arms, the U.S. fleet is less than half the size it was a decade ago. It is spread too thin to cover all possible crisis spots simultaneously, and it is incapable, its leaders assert, of winning battles in many places where it may be called upon to wage them. The Navy's readiness, says Vice-Admiral M. Staser Holcomb, the Navy's planning director, "is at a 30-year low."

This is why a dramatic buildup of U.S. sea power has emerged as the dominant goal in the Reagan Administration's plans for huge increases in military spending. Weinberger may decide that the cost of the B-1 bomber cannot be justified, and he could elect to scale back the size and cost of the MX missile system. But he says firmly that the Navy will get the lion's share of the $1.65 trillion for defense that President Reagan plans to ask for from 1983 to 1987. This would increase the Navy's fleet to 600 ships, compared with today's 456 ships.

[2] Reprint of a magazine article "Building a Navy to Rule the Seas Again," by the staff of *Business Week*. pp. 171–80. Jl. 20, '81. Reprinted from the July 20, 1981 issue of *Business Week* by special permission. Copyright © 1981 by McGraw-Hill, Inc., New York, N.Y. 10020. All rights reserved.

The $70 billion shipbuilding program that is being planned through 1987 (table) centers on construction of two more Nimitz-class nuclear-powered aircraft carriers and the formation of three additional carrier battle groups. The Navy wants big carriers because they are the only ships that can carry F-14 and F-18 fighter aircraft.

Criticism. But critics charge this is the wrong way to go. Building three new 91,000-ton nuclear carriers—and all the cruisers, destroyers, frigates, attack submarines, aircraft, and cruise missiles to defend them—would be very expensive. The Nimitz-class carriers now cost $3.5 billion each to build and would be inviting targets for Russian cruise missiles that can be launched against them at ranges of up to 200 mi., critics claim. Among the most outspoken is Senator Gary W. Hart (D-Colo.) of the Senate Armed Services Committee, who maintains that "the big-carrier approach will cause the U.S. to build the wrong kinds of ships and end up with a weaker Navy in the future." To decrease its present vulnera-

The Navy's five-year shipbuilding plans

	Under Carter	Under Reagan	Contractor
	Fiscal 1982–86	Fiscal 1983–87	
Aircraft carriers	0	?	Newport News
Nimitz class			
Cruisers	16	17	Litton
Aegis CG-47 class			
Destroyers	0	6	Litton
DD-963 class			
Frigates	1	9	Todd or Bath
FFG-7 class			
Submarines			
Attack, SSN-688 class .	7	14	Newport News
Ballistic missile,			or
Trident class	5	7	Electric Boat
Support ships			
Amphibious	0	9	
Oilers, ammunition ...	7	23	Undecided
All other	49	63	
Total	**85**	**150**	

bility, Hart would have the Navy build smaller, oil-fired carriers in greater numbers, equip their support ships with vertical-takeoff Harrier aircraft, and disperse such battle groups widely around the world.

For the present, few are heeding Hart's complaints. Two years ago, Congress ordered a fourth Nimitz-class carrier over the veto of former President Carter. This year it will approve the Reagan Administration's request to begin building a fifth, with at least one other to follow.

But if the nation's economy does not improve or if demand builds up for greater social spending, opposition will erupt and will be echoed by complaints from the other services. The Administration's projections for its defense budgets through 1987 leave no doubt that attaining naval superiority will come at the expense of other military procurement, and the services now know how much. In a confidential five-year defense budget and planning directive, distributed in mid-June, Weinberger allocated $512 billion to the Navy, compared with $487 billion to the Air Force, $372 billion to the Army, and $282 billion to other Defense Dept. agencies. Shipbuilding gets one-sixth of the Navy's $512 billion. And the cost of adding three more battle groups is pegged at $45 billion.

Administration officials deny that the Navy has become their policymaking pet. "In terms of military policy," declares William Schneider Jr., the Office of Management & Budget's associate director for national security, "we are not emphasizing the Navy any more heavily than we are Air Force tactical air power." But Schneider concedes that "in terms of resources, the Navy will be the heaviest claimant to Defense Dept. money because we need a lot of costly capital ships as fast as we can get them."

The front-runner. Pentagon insiders cite a less obvious reason for the Navy's front-running position: the persuasiveness of Navy Secretary John F. Lehman Jr. in top-level Defense Dept. planning councils. "Lehman is riding roughshod over the Army and the Air Force," declares one Pentagon source. "He hit the ground running over here. He knows exactly what he wants and how to get it."

Lehman wants a three-ocean U.S. fleet potent enough to beard the Soviet navy in what are generally considered its home waters—the Norwegian Sea, the eastern Mediterranean, and the Sea of Japan. Made up of at least 15 carrier battle groups instead of the present 12, this expanded U.S. naval force could deploy at least two battle groups in the Pacific, the Indian Ocean, and the Atlantic-Mediterranean area at all times.

Support for such a plan has been growing since 1979, when the Navy dispatched two carrier battle groups to the Arabian Sea during the Iranian hostage crisis and continued patrolling there during the Soviet invasion of Afghanistan and the threat of its intervention in Iran. It had to pirate battle groups for this patrolling action from both its Mediterranean and Pacific forces, leaving these areas largely underdefended. "We are attempting to cover three oceans with a one-and-a-half ocean Navy," says Lehman. "It's like pulling a too-small sheet from one side of the bed to the other."

According to Lehman, the Navy's forces have diminished in recent years because previous Presidents, notably Carter, downgraded the Navy's importance. "The 30-day war in Europe used to be the name of the game," he maintains. "The theory was that we would either bring the Soviets to a standstill within that time or we would lose the war. The Navy couldn't help much. Thus putting more money into ships wasn't worth it."

Under the Reagan Administration's plans for global naval power, the strategy is entirely different. "We are going to change from a pulled-back strategy that had the Navy operating only in low-threat areas to one in which it will be expected to operate in high-threat areas close to the Soviet Union," says Lehman. "We will expect the U.S. Navy to be able to bottle up the Russian fleet and defeat it if it threatens U.S. access to the sea-lanes anywhere."

The Soviet navy, explains U.S. Chief of Naval Operations

Thomas B. Hayward, "is now coming into the seas of the world in ways we thought impossible only a few years ago." It is deploying technologically sophisticated cruisers, destroyers, and amphibious ships. Half of its missile-armed, intercontinental-range Backfire bombers are now assigned to sea patrol. Even more ominous, it has started deploying cruise missiles aboard attack submarines that are as large as the new U.S. Trident submarines; it is starting to deploy a titanium-hulled attack submarine that can outdive U.S. subs; and it has a ballistic-missile submarine much quieter and harder to detect than its predecessors.

Long timetables. Such developments, "which terrify me," says one high-level Pentagon official, lie behind the Reagan Administration's demand for a strong Navy. But the buildup cannot come all that quickly. The Navy has ordered Honeywell Inc. to step up development of an advanced, lightweight homing torpedo, designed to dive much deeper and go much faster than any torpedo now in the U.S. arsenal. But it will not be ready until the late 1980s. Also under development is a submarine-fired missile that will be able to fly several hundred miles, then dive back into the sea and home in

**The Navy's current
top contractors**

Company	Dollar value of contracts awarded Oct. 1, 1980, though Mar. 31, 1981 (millions of dollars)
McDonnell Douglas	$1,393
Grumman	919
General Dynamics	859
General Electric	598
United Technologies	450
Sperry Rand	376
Hughes Aircraft	376
Lockheed	344
Litton Industries	336
Westinghouse	302

Data: Naval Material Command

on enemy subs just as a conventional torpedo does. This weapon, too, is several years from production.

Shipbuilding plans also are long term. Construction of a nuclear carrier takes about seven years and building most other major surface ships requires four to five years. So the 18 major ships that will get startup money in the Navy's $10.3 billion budget for fiscal 1982 will not be in service until the latter half of the 1980s. And operation of all 143 ships that the Navy is now proposing to contract for through fiscal 1987 will not be possible until the early 1990s.

Lehman chafes at such long timetables. He sees grave dangers for the U.S. during the next half-dozen years, and that is why he wants to put back into service at least two old battleships, starting with the *New Jersey*, and one or two old carriers, starting with the *Oriskany*. The price of reactivating this firepower could be $1 billion.

Congress likes the battleship idea. The *New Jersey*'s 16-in. guns are still the most devastating nonnuclear weapons that can be fired at a land target from the sea. The old battleship is about as fast as modern U.S. frigates and cruisers and is less vulnerable because of its 14 in. of heavy steel armor plating. And it can be outfitted in 21 months to carry up to 50 long-range Tomahawk and Harpoon cruise missiles.

Cruise missiles will make the *New Jersey* such a powerful weapon, says Lehman, that "we may even build a separate battle group around it." This would include, in the fashion of future U.S. battle groups, CG-47 cruisers equipped with Aegis computer-controlled, missile-firing defense systems. The first CG-47, the $1.25 billion *Ticonderoga*, was christened in mid-June. Litton Industries Inc. has another under construction, and at least 17 more are planned through 1987.

The Navy also wants to put cruise missiles on surface ships, as well as on many of the 100 nuclear-powered attack submarines it expects to have on station by 1990. Both General Dynamics Corp., which makes the Tomahawk, and McDonnell Douglas Corp., manufacturer of the Harpoon, can turn out several thousand missiles relatively quickly as soon as contracts are signed.

Shipyard improvements. In Congress, the Navy's plans for cruise missiles have raised little opposition. Only in its proposal to reactivate the *Oriskany* has the Navy been refused funds in fiscal 1982. That happened, says Lehman, because restoring the old carrier could cut into contracting funds that the shipbuilding industry and its friends in Congress would prefer to put into new ships. "There is evidence that some contractors bad-mouthed the idea," he claims.

Contractors are more enthusiastic about the Navy's other plans. In fact, they are trying to convince both the Administration and Congress that, despite a poor performance record over the past few years, they can handle the Navy's new contracts in fine style. They now need new contracts to avoid layoffs, they say. And a few companies have even increased spending recently to improve shipyard productivity.

Anticipating questions about the capability of U.S. shipyards to provide a 600-ship Navy, Lehman sent Weinberger a classified memorandum on May 28 in which he cited nearly $150 million in capital improvements in U.S. shipyards that should permit a surge in Navy work. More such investments are in the offing. Newport News Shipbuilding Co., for example, plans to spend $400 million over the next five years to improve and expand its facilities. Lehman asked Weinberger to relay this "firmness of resolve by private industry" to Presi-

Today's U.S. fleet
vs. the Soviet Union's

Ships in operation	U.S.	Soviet
Aircraft carriers	13	2
Cruisers and destroyers	122	103
Frigates	71	168
Submarines	119	372
Amphibious	66	86
Logistics	73	150
Mine warfare	25	165
Patrol	3	120
Other support	39	610
Total	531	1,776

dent Reagan because "our momentum needs [Reagan's] unstinting support."

Manpower deficiencies. The Navy also wants to make sure that there are enough subcontractors to produce the critical materials needed by the shipyards. Many have left the shipbuilding supply business over the past 10 years. So the Navy has compiled a list not only of what components it will need and on what timetable but also who can supply them. Robert H. Link, the Naval Sea System Command's executive director for acquisition, admits that "some balancing will have to be done" to square the pace of contractors' orders with their production timetables. He sees a more serious problem in Navy manpower deficiencies. A minimum of 1,000 additional engineering supervisors will have to be added to the 4,100 the Navy now has in contractors' facilities, says Link, and 2,000 will have to be added to the 4,600 now in Washington. But Congress has set limits on the number of these supervisors and, given the Administration's holddown on new hiring, it is hard to see how their ranks can be increased.

The prospect of an additional armada of Navy supervisors peering over its shoulder does not appeal to the industry. Even worse, it suggests that the Navy is worried about an old problem—production contracts that come apart because of change orders, cost escalations, and other hassles between the Navy and the shipyards that end up in bitter settlement battles and poor-quality ships.

In trying to establish better relations with its Navy contractors, the Reagan Administration did not get off to an auspicious start. In fact, it appeared that it was seeking trouble in its decision to cancel competition between General Dynamics' Electric Boat Div. and Newport News, a subsidiary of Tenneco Inc., for a contract to build three new attack subs last May. Secretary Lehman admits he was angered by "serious problems of quality control at Electric Boat." He dealt the yard out of the bidding and awarded the contract to Newport News, which, he said, "had not had a submarine contract since 1978 and faced a serious erosion of its ship-producing base."

'Neanderthal' contracting? Electric Boat protested, and Newport News has refused to sign the contract it was offered. The reason: Navy insistence that, as part of the deal, Newport News must identify any possible cost overruns within nine months of signing the contract.

Newport News President Edward J. Campbell says that such a restriction would preempt his shipyard's rights. For one thing, he points out, Newport News would be asked to use a good deal of government-furnished equipment in building the attack subs and would not be ready to put much of it into the new craft until a year or more after construction had started. If such equipment turns out to be defective, which is too often the case, "who is going to pay us for production time lost waiting for replacements?" asks Campbell.

An executive of one company that deals with all three branches of the military calls the Navy "Neanderthal" in its contracting and suggests that if it does not change its ways quickly its expanded shipbuilding plans "just won't happen." Relationships between the Navy and shipbuilders will remain sour, others suggest, as long as Admiral Hyman G. Rickover, the Navy's nuclear shipbuilding boss, stays on the job. The 81-year-old Rickover has long accused shipbuilders of doing shoddy work, padding claims, and gross underbidding. In May, he asked Congress to permit the Navy to ignore low bids on ships if it believes such bids are deliberate buy-ins.

Other Navy officials are convinced that the success of their program will depend on "selective allocation" of major ship contracts to yards experienced in building such craft: Litton for destroyers and Aegis-equipped cruisers, Todd Shipyards and Bath Iron Works for frigates, and Newport News for nuclear carriers. Thus, competition may be restricted to contracts for support ships such as amphibious and supply vessels.

The Navy plans to contract for 95 such vessels through 1987. This should mean big business for Bethlehem Steel's shipyard at Sparrows Point, Md., General Dynamics' yard at Quincy, Mass., Ogden Corp.'s Avondale yard at New Orleans, National Steel's at San Diego, and Lockheed's in Seattle.

There is even a chance that one or more Navy shipyards, such as Mare Island, Calif., will be activated to help build ships. But this could create more discord with industry, and the Navy may already have too much to do in dealing with its contractors.

"Frankly, I don't think the Navy's shipbuilding program is manageable in the time frame it has set for it," says one key congressional military affairs staffer. Adds another: "When Weinberger assesses the demands of the other services, the sheer costs will force him to start cutting shipbuilding, too."

Any such cutting would have to begin with the supercarriers, because the rest of the fleet is built around them. That will open up challenges from Congress, particularly from Senator William Proxmire (D-Wis.), who already thinks the total price tag for each new carrier battle group could be more than $30 billion, double what the Navy claims. "And what will we get?" he asks. "A large floating target for advanced Soviet missiles—like hitting a bull in the butt with a bass fiddle."

AMERICA NEEDS SMALL CARRIERS[3]

Some distinguished naval officers maintain that the United States needs big carriers. Their argument is that only big carriers can effectively and safely handle the type of aircraft which the Navy has and will have for at least the next decade. I certainly would not dispute that. But I would take exception as to whether the Navy should plan on continuing with these same types of aircraft by the time the next U.S. carriers can be built and join the fleet—which is about a decade from now.

Here we need to look at the purposes for having aircraft at sea. The first is to intercept and shoot down enemy aircraft

[3] Reprint of a newspaper article "America needs small carriers," by Admiral Stansfield Turner, former head of the U.S. Central Intelligence Agency. *The Christian Science Monitor*. p. 22. Ag. 12, '81. Copyright © 1981 by Stansfield Turner. Reprinted by permission.

or missiles that are threatening U.S. forces at sea. The second is to drop bombs or launch missiles at targets on land.

An example of the first type of aircraft is the Navy's fabled F-14. There are few other aircraft in the world that have better air combat maneuvering capability than this one. It can tangle and dogfight with the best of them. It also carries a superb radar and a missile named Phoenix which can be launched at an enemy aircraft as far as 60 miles away. Clearly one does not need the high maneuverability for dogfighting when attacking another aircraft at a distance of 60 miles.

In short, the U.S. has paid twice for maneuverability in this weapons system—once in the airframe and once in the missile. That is understandable because the F-14 is in fact clear evidence of a transition that is taking place in the tactics of fighting in the air. We are moving from the traditional dogfighting mode to one of reliance on sophisticated missiles that can outdogfight any aircraft. When that day comes, and it should come very quickly if the Navy and the Air Force will pay attention, the need for very high performance aircraft will disappear.

So, too, will the requirement for a big aircraft carrier to mother them. Vertical takeoff aircraft that are fast though not highly maneuverable, but equipped with highly capable missiles, will replace the F-14 in this air superiority role. They, in turn, can be launched not only from very small aircraft carriers but from all manner of small ships.

The role of launching weapons from aircraft against ground targets is also in transition. Toward the end of the war in Vietnam the U.S. began to use "smart" bombs and missiles. The capabilities of these weapons far exceeded the traditional iron bombs of wars past.

Equally importantly, the U.S. is going to need to utilize stand-off missiles to attack ground targets because of the increasing threat to aircraft from anti-aircraft defenses. One of the technological revolutions in recent years has been great improvement in anti-air guns and missiles. Few military strategists today believe than manned aircraft can operate in a high threat environment without unacceptable losses.

If, then, the U.S. is going to utilize aircraft to support troops on the ground or to destroy heavily defended installations on the ground, it will have to keep the aircraft itself out of range of the most intense anti-air fire. That means launching a long-range guided missile to the target. Again, there is no need for a high performance aircraft to carry the smart missile to the periphery of danger. Almost any aircraft can do it.

The counter argument is that we still need the benefit of a man's eyesight over the target to make last-minute decisions. Today's technology, however, will enable us to surveil almost any point on the earth with unmanned drones that are so small and maneuverable that they would be difficult to destroy. Such a drone could send back all the information wanted as to what is going on in the area of the target. It could send back television pictures, data gathered from infrared sensors, and radar images. The data can be digested by human beings in remote locations even better than by a pilot in a cockpit. In turn these human beings can direct the smart stand-off missiles that are being launched from the low-performance aircraft. So, again, a big carrier will not be necessary to accommodate the attack aircraft.

There are, of course, various other kinds of support aircraft on aircraft carriers. Some carry search radars, some carry antisubmarine equipment. Most of these would fit on small carriers today or certainly could be scaled down to do so in the future. In point of fact the most important mission for carriers in the future will be to carry these radar aircraft which will be needed in large numbers. The interceptor and attack aircraft in the vertical take-off mode can be accommodated on all manner of ships.

Beyond this the Navy must be looking today at alternatives to aircraft and aircraft carriers. One possibility is the long-range cruise missile. This can be put on almost any ship or submarine for use against targets on the shore. In turn almost any surface ship can launch a remotely piloted drone aircraft that can be the eyes and ears to turn the cruise missile into a lethal weapon against even a moving target. In short, the Navy's firepower is going to proliferate to all manner of ships rather than being concentrated in a dozen large and vulnerable supercarriers.

A final point of concern is vulnerability. Size brings more disadvantages of vulnerability today than advantages of capability for defense. Size, or mass, means that a large aircraft carrier is going to be detected more easily by whatever form of detector the enemy uses. Size means that the enemy's smart weapons are going to be able to distinguish which is the carrier and which is the tanker or merchant ship or destroyer more readily. Size means that efforts to use electronic wizardry to deceive or decoy an incoming missile will be much more difficult since it will be nearly impossible to create the illusion that the aircraft carrier is somewhere other than it really is.

The pendulum of offense and defense constantly swings back and forth in the military world. Today it is definitely inclining on the side of the attacker against ships at sea. Technology is making the weapons of defense smaller and more lethal. Someday the pendulum will swing back, but in the meantime we can put on small carriers almost as much lethality for defense as on large ones without having to accept the handicap of greatly increased vulnerability that goes with size.

Proponents of big carriers are right in saying that we are stuck for the moment with such carriers to handle large, heavy, and high-performance aircraft, but any new aircraft carrier that the U.S. builds will be with us for 30 or perhaps 40 years. Surely we must have the vision to ask whether the supercarrier will be a viable weapons system that far into the future.

I believe it will not. Moreover, I believe that we will not need or want such a weapons system when the world of high technology is giving us far more capable ones to do the same tasks. If we do not take advantage of these emerging technologies and move into them well ahead of the Soviet Navy, American seapower is bound to be eclipsed by the tremendous effort and expense which the Soviets are putting into

their navy. The U.S. has the technology and the cleverness to
stay ahead, but to do that it must break with the supercarrier
and move into the realm of the future.

PROTECTING U.S. INTERESTS IN THE PERSIAN GULF REGION[4]

The 1970s closed with the Soviet invasion of Afghanistan.
The 1980s opened with the ensuing debate, both in this country and around the world, about how to respond to the invasion. At times confused, at times angry, at times profound,
this debate is not yet resolved.

In my remarks today, I want to talk about U.S. interests—
some of them vital—in that part of the world, about the nature of the challenge presented by the Soviet threat there,
about our response to that challenge, and particularly about
how our military capabilities fit into an overall security policy
framework for the region and contribute to that response.

While recent events in Afghanistan are of critical significance, they are by no means the entire problem. Any discussion of the appropriate U.S. response must begin by placing
these specific events—the invasion and its consequences—in
the broader context of historical and possible or likely future
developments.

The full context of the Soviet invasion includes historical
Russian ambitions in that region, a 20-year buildup of Soviet
military forces, the more recent development of Soviet power
projection capabilities, and the very recent upheavals in the
Islamic world.

Interpretations of the reasons for the Soviet invasion vary.
The simple fact is that their motives are very likely to be
mixed, and we don't know the exact mixture. But policymakers cannot avoid dealing with both the specific inci-

[4] Reprint of a speech by President Carter's Secretary of Defense, Harold R.
Brown, before the Council on Foreign Relations in New York City, March 6, 1980.
Department of State Bulletin. 80:63–7. My. '80.

dent—the invasion—and the longer range question of how to deter such actions in the future. Reflecting this, the U.S. response since the December invasion has been on two levels:

Extracting a real price from the Soviets for this specific case of outright aggression and

Continuing to design a strategy and to develop a set of economic, political, diplomatic, and military measures to deter or defeat similar Soviet moves in the future—moves that could more directly threaten U.S. interests.

U.S. Interests

U.S. interests related to the Persian Gulf-southwest Asian region, certainly in the short term, focus on the safe and speedy release of the Americans held hostage in Tehran. For the longer term, our interests can be stated quite simply:

To insure access to adequate oil supplies;

To resist Soviet expansion;

To promote stability in the region; and

To advance the Middle East peace process, while insuring—and, indeed, in order to help insure—the continued security of the State of Israel.

Let us look more closely at each of these in turn.

Oil is the lifeblood of modern industrial societies. Sixty percent of the world's imported petroleum comes from this region: about 13% of the oil consumed in the United States and much higher percentages for our allies—45% for Germany and 75% for France and for Japan.

The loss of this oil to the economies of the West and the industrialized Far East would be a blow of catastrophic proportions.

Even given success in the much needed effort to reduce American dependence on imported oil, the loss of Persian Gulf supplies would do irreparable damage to our allies and friends. In fact, Soviet control of this area would make virtual economic vassals of much of both the industrialized and the less developed worlds. The U.S.S.R. would not even need actually to interrupt the flow of oil.

Russian dreams and schemes of expansion and dominion in this region go back to Tsarist days. But our long term interests, and those of the area, are best served if the countries of that region are free to develop in their own ways, not subject to foreign pressure of domination. Putting Soviet power astride vast oil resources would, for the first time, give the Soviet state international economic leverage on a par with its military might.

Stability in the region does not mean the absence of change. It does require a strong measure of security for each of its states and opportunities for the nonviolent resolution of local tensions and differences. The influences of both the industrialized West and Islamic fundamentalism will continue to touch directly the lives of individuals and the future of nations in that region. But there is a role for us to play in building individual and collective local security, while at the same time discouraging such destabilizing developments as the proliferation of nuclear weapons.

The Middle East peace process is a fundamental component of U.S. policy as is our commitment to the security of Israel. These aspects of striving for a stable and secure Middle East have taken on new significance in the wake of the recent events in Iran and Afghanistan.

The road to peace in the Middle East is long, steep, and hazardous. But progress along that road has been—viewed overall—one of the great success stories in international affairs. In 1973 Israel and Egypt were at war. When this Administration took office, the only international exchanges between the two nations came from the barrels of guns used in border attacks.

In 3 short years, we have witnessed the Camp David accords, the frameworks for a comprehensive peace, and open borders and exchanges of ambassadors. In pursuing peace we will continue to honor our national commitment to the security of Israel. We will also work with our Arab friends to pro-

vide a security framework that helps protect the region from
Soviet expansionism and any consequent threats to the free
flow of oil which is so important to them and the rest of the
world.

As we seek to advance these four interests, our determination to respond to any threat to them is clear. As President
Carter said in his State of the Union speech: "An attempt by
any outside force to gain control of the Persian Gulf region
will be regarded as an assault on the vital interests of the
United States of America, and such an assault will be repelled
by any means necessary, including military force."

International Complications for the Soviets

Before I elaborate on our strategy and capabilities to
deter any such threat in the future, I would like to outline
several other factors which compound Soviet calculations in
the area and could contribute to the solution of our problems
there.

First and foremost of these is the resurgence of Islam,
reinforcing an historic trend toward nationalism in that part
of the world. Unlike the Soviet Union, we are not seeking to
insulate a large Islamic population from the influences of
their religious tradition. We do not seek to suppress religious
activism in the Islamic world. And this is true even with respect to Iran. As we have made clear many times during the
continuing hostage crisis, if there is an external threat to
Iran's Islamic revolution, it comes from the Soviet Union, not
from the United States.

Second, and related to the first, is the active resistance of
nationalistic peoples to outside domination. Recent events in
Afghanistan remind us—and, more immediately no doubt,
the Soviets—of the timeless truth of Toynbee's description of
the classic problem of invaders:

. . . an overweening self-confidence, bred by this mistaken belief in
their own invincibility, then leads them on to court disaster by
rashly attacking still unbroken peoples whose spirit and capacity
for resistance takes them by surprise.

I do not mean to imply that the Soviets cannot prevail in Afghanistan. They can—but only at a price, and it is a steep one. And whatever problems the forces of religion and independence which are sweeping the area create for us, let us not forget that ultimately they can help inhibit Soviet expansionism.

Third World concerns have played what is to some observers a surprising role in the aftermath of the Soviet invasion. Afghanistan had been friendly, indeed pro-Soviet. An underdeveloped nation, it historically has been a buffer state between great power rivals. The swift dispatch of Soviet tanks, helicopter gunships, and tens of thousands of troops to suppress "friendly" Afghanistan rightly shocked much of the Third World.

Our allies and the other industrialized democracies—and, to take a different example, China as well—share our interests and concerns in the area—and, by and large, our evaluation of the dangers—even if they do not accept every element of our formulas for dealing with the situation. Western Europe and Japan, even more than we, depend on the oil resources of the region. Many of our allies have historic ties to countries there.

While we seek allied support in the region, we must realize that direct contributions are not the only way they can help. For example, increased allied contributions to their own security provide us greater flexibility in the measures we must take to bolster our military capabilities for meeting threats to the peace and our common interests in the Persian Gulf and southwest Asia.

These diverse factors can help us meet the challenge posed by the Soviets—indeed, they are an indispensable part of the total response. Nonetheless, there is no doubt that the United States must take the lead in organizing a comprehensive response to Soviet aggression in Afghanistan and must be an effective deterrent to still more dangerous actions they might otherwise be tempted to take in the future. This comprehensive response must have many facets—military and nonmilitary.

Nonmilitary Components of Deterrence

The first nonmilitary ingredient is an effective, long term energy policy to reduce our dependence on imported oil. This objective is crucial to our national security in the future.

However, it must also be clearly understood that no conceivable combination of measures—conservation, stockpiling, or alternate energy sources—can totally eliminate the near term security problem that is created by threats to the gulf and its oil. The hard fact is that there is nothing the United States—or our industrial world partners or the less developed countries—can do in the coming decade, or probably even the next, that would save us from severe damage if the bulk of the oil supply from the Persian Gulf were cut off for a sustained period.

The issue here is not, as some have claimed, one of going to war for the Organization of Petroleum Exporting Countries or to avoid waiting in gas lines. Conservation is necessary in any event. But to advocate it as a substitute for U.S. leadership in strengthening the security of the area is simply to fail to grasp, or to wish away, the gravity of the true situation, as it affects not only us but our allies and friends. Even an energy self-sufficient America would not be secure in a world in which Western Europe or Japan or Turkey or Brazil could be made energy hostages of a hostile power.

The second nonmilitary aspect is economic assistance to those countries in the region that are grappling with the problems of development. A particularly important example is the case of our ally Turkey. Economic uncertainty tends to fuel political instability. Helping a country solve its internal problems enables it to deal more effectively with common security and other regional concerns. We look to our friends in the industrialized world and to the wealthy oil producers in the area to bear their full share of this part of the task.

Military Components of Deterrence

Let me turn now to the military components. In our military planning for the Persian Gulf and the southwest Asia—

as indeed across the board—our first objective is to deter; that is, we seek to make clear that there will be major risks and penalities associated with aggression. We must be able, if need be, to defeat aggression at various levels. Without question, such an ability and the will to use it constitute the most effective deterrent.

Before I move on to discuss the kinds of forces that are necessary to carry out this objective, let me make four general observations about the military components of our response.

First, while the terms "rapid deployment forces" and "power projection" are relatively new additions to the jargon, the military missions they signify are not new at all. The United States has been in the rapid deployment and power projection business for a long time. If you doubt that, ask the Marines who 5 years ago celebrated their 200th anniversary.

In both World Wars, in Korea, and then in Vietnam, we showed that we were able to sustain very large military forces very far from our shores. Whatever our other difficulties in those cases, the logistics capability which the United States demonstrated was impressive indeed. Moreover, it has long been a part of our military doctrine to be ready to engage in contingencies in remote areas, without unacceptably compromising our ability to maintain deterrence and defense in other theaters.

Second, I reject altogether the proposition that we should not develop the capability to use military forces effectively because we might then be tempted to use them unwisely. I believe the American people and their political and military leaders are wise enough—and, one might add, experienced enough—to understand and accept a few simple truths.

—Military forces alone cannot solve all the world's problems.
—Their commitment is a very serious business.
—Such forces and the will to use them when necessary are essential to the defense of our vital interests.
—Those interests must be carefully defined.

We must be guided by the lessons of history and not haunted by its ghosts.

Third, there have been some press reports of alleged U.S. reliance on a "trip wire" strategy, in which we would, by preference or necessity, quickly resort to theater nuclear weapons to defend against Soviet attack in the area. Several points need to be made. Any direct conflict between American and Soviet forces carries the risk of intensification and geographical spread of the conflict. We cannot concede to the Soviets full choice of the arena or the actions.

But that by no means implies that escalation to the use of nuclear weapons will be the consequence of a U.S.–Soviet clash in southwest Asia. In part to make such a result less likely, a major portion of our effort in the region is devoted to improving the conventional strength we can bring to bear there. In fact, given U.S. capabilities and those of others whose interests would be threatened by Soviet aggression, given the difficulties inherent in any Soviet military actions beyond its borders in rugged terrain and hostile surroundings, and given our wide range of options both to exploit other Soviet vulnerabilities and to defend against attack, conventional deterrence and defense are feasible goals.

My fourth general observation is that this overall response is, and must be, a multilateral one, involving local forces, U.S. forces, and those of other countries outside the region. For example, we are working with several countries in the region for increased U.S. access to local facilities. We are talking with both potential contributors and potential recipients concerning programs of economic support and security assistance—which are necessary complements to our other efforts. And we are consulting with countries both in the region and outside concerning military cooperation there.

Despite the complexities inherent in multilateral action by independent nations, on the whole we have been quite successful in our endeavors, and we expect this to continue. I should note that in many instances, we seek not formal, public guarantees and agreements but rather the establishment of a pattern of quiet consultation and parallel pursuit of common security goals.

Meeting the objective of deterrence will require a combination of local forces for self-defense, U.S. forces present in the area, and, as appropriate, U.S. and other forces capable of rapid deployment to reinforce threatened areas.

In most cases—indeed, to some degree in all cases—local forces in a country under attack or directly threatened would mobilize for its defense. We cannot hope, nor do we plan, to defend peoples in the region who will not help defend themselves. By that same token, where we are involved, we do not expect to stand alone. Because aggression against one could spread to threaten all, others in the regions may well—and surely ought to—join in the collective defense. The kinds of assistance they would contribute would vary greatly from case to case, ranging from providing necessary access and support facilities to mobilizing forces that would stand alongside our own to deter and engage an enemy.

In addition to indigenous forces, deterrence involves both U.S. military presence in a troubled region and U.S. forces which can be quickly moved to it. What is important is the ability rapidly to move forces into the region with the numbers, mobility, and firepower to preclude initial adversary forces from reaching vital points. It is not necessary for our initial units to be able to defeat the whole force an adversary might eventually have in place. It is also not necessary for us to await the firing of the first shot or the prior arrival of hostile forces; many of our forces can be moved upon strategic warning and some upon receipt of even very early and ambiguous indications.

An effective U.S. response to aggression in this or other troublespots consists of several ingredients. The first—an enhanced continuing peacetime presence—will involve primarily naval forces. Our current naval power in the region is greatly superior to that of the Soviet Union in the area. It provides us with an immediate tactical air capability. I might add that the French also have a powerful naval force in the Indian Ocean. Further, we are continuing to make improvements, begun several years ago, in the facilities on Diego Garcia. We will have a permanent presence in the region that is much greater than it was a year ago.

Prepositioning of equipment is the vital second ingredient. We have begun a program to procure a number of
maritime prepositioning ships, which will give us greater flexibility and avoid the problems of large, permanent U.S. bases
overseas in sensitive areas.

As a near term option, we are now actively assembling a
seven-ship force of commercial-type vessels, including roll-
on, roll-off ships, break-bulk cargo ships, and tankers to provide us with this capability within the next several months.
These ships will be loaded with unit equipment, supplies,
fuel, and water that would enable a Marine amphibious brigade of some 10,000 men, as well as several U.S. Air Force
fighter squadrons, to operate until further logistic support can
arrive from the United States.

The loaded ships will be prepositioned within a few days'
sailing distance of the Persian Gulf-Arabian Sea area. In an
emergency they could move to a designated port near the objective and join up there with personnel and planes flown
directly from U.S. bases. This arrangement will provide us the
capability of responding to a crisis in the area in days rather
than weeks.

Mobility—especially air and sealift capabilities—is the
third ingredient. We are not without such capabilities today.
For example, the first land-based tactical aircraft could be in
the region in a matter of hours and significant units backed up
by AWACS [airborne warning and control system] within a
few days. The first battalion of the 82nd Airborne Division
could arrive within 48 hours of a movement order; the entire
division could close in in about 2 weeks. A full Marine amphibious force (one division and air wing) could be deployed
in 4 weeks.

Moreover, we are now programing major improvements
to our rapid deployment capabilities. Several years ago, we
started procurement of KC-10 aerial tankers, and we are now
accelerating our purchases. We have also begun a long-term
program for procurement of a new "CX" transport aircraft—
either of new design or based on an existing aircraft—for

long-distance deployment of out-sized cargos. We are also, as an interim measure, in the process of acquiring high-speed civilian ships which have immediate military sealift potential.

Fourth is the access and transit rights which I alluded to earlier. We are intensively—and I judge successfully—negotiating increased access to port, airfield, and other facilities to improve our ability to sustain naval and aircraft deployments.

Let me again emphasize the difference between seeking access and seeking permanent bases. Essentially, we are asking various countries in the area to enable us to come more effectively to their assistance if and when they need and want us. This is far different from asking them to host permanent U.S. garrisons.

Frequent deployment and exercises in the area comprise another key ingredient. We have increased the scale and pace of our periodic naval task force deployments in the region.

For example, to take a specific point in time, last October the U.S.S. *Midway* carrier battle group was conducting an exercise in the Indian Ocean with naval units from the United Kingdom and Australia. Additionally, four ships of the U.S. Mideast force were on station in the Persian Gulf. A second aircraft carrier battle group from the western Pacific arrived in the Arabian Sea in December. Since that time, more than 150 carrier-based tactical aircraft and 14 warships have been continuously available in the Persian Gulf and Arabian Sea to maintain a visible U.S. presence.

Our ability to project air power at extended distances has been further demonstrated by three B-52 sea surveillance and three airborne warning and control missions flown in the Indian Ocean area. Finally, a Marine amphibious unit will arrive in the Arabian Sea later this month. And even earlier, we deployed tactical aircraft there—for example, F-15s and AWACS to Saudi Arabia—as part of our response to the threat to North Yemen.

In the debate growing out of the Persian Gulf crisis, we seem sometimes to labor under attack from a curious combination of critics. On the one hand, there are those who pound the podium and call for ill-defined tough measures—often to cure problems for which there is no military solution—while at the same time deriding our military capabilities. On the other hand, different voices declare that we face no real problems except those created by our own overreaction and thus need not be concerned about our military capabilities.

Adopting either attitude as our nation's policy would leave our security in great hazard and would give a seriously and dangerously wrong signal to the Soviet Union.

Conclusion

The policies and the approach I have outlined are not steps toward war. They are designed to build strength and to prevent war. What we are doing constitutes a necessary and reasonable response to real needs. The massive growth of Soviet military capabilities is a fact. Their willingness to use surrogates and, indeed, units of the Red Army to assert military and political power outside the borders of the Soviet Union has been demonstrated. The United States and the nations to which we have the closest ties are now, and will be for a long time, linked by a highly vulnerable lifeline to the Middle East and the Persian Gulf.

Perhaps the Soviets will never move to threaten that lifeline. Perhaps the more "benign" interpretations of their invasion of Afghanistan—if the word "benign" can be used at all—are correct. But, as policymakers and as responsible citizens and world leaders, we cannot safely assume that it is. Indeed, the actions that we must take to guard against the consequences of the immediate threat posed by recent aggressive Soviet behavior are probably the most effective way to moderate future Soviet actions over the long term.

We are not saying to the Soviet Union that competition is the only path between us. We remain willing to cooperate in those areas where our interests overlap, as in the case of SALT. But where they threaten our interests, we will meet them on that ground as well.

We must demonstrate to the Soviet Union that:

—The invasion of Afghanistan is seen, throughout that part of the world that is not ruled from Moscow, as a callous violation of the norms of international behavior;

—Their stated justification for it is universally regarded as a transparent misrepresentation; and

—The international community believes that similar steps in the future carry the gravest dangers for the Soviets as well as for the rest of us.

For the United States to assume its proper role in deterring such aggression in the future, we must have adequate military capability and the will to use it if necessary. If we intend to remain a major world power, and to preserve our own pluralistic and economic systems, then we must engage over the long haul in an economic rebuilding, a program to reduce our dependence on imported energy, and, not least, an enhancement of our military capability, including an ability to deploy forces rapidly to areas far from but vital to us, in a security framework that helps to stabilize such regions.

These tasks will not be easy. They cannot be done as a one-time crash program. They will not be inexpensive. But if we fail to carry them out, the 21st century will be a dangerous one indeed for our ideals, for our society, and for our children.

AMERICA ENGULFED[5]

The United States has taken on a major new global commitment: to preserve access to the Persian Gulf for the West. President Carter accepted this commitment on January 23, 1980, in the wake of the fall of Shah Mohammad Reza Pahlavi of Iran and the Soviet invasion of Afghanistan. "An attempt by any outside force to gain control of the Persian Gulf region," he asserted, "will be regarded as an assault on the

[5] Reprint of a magazine article, "America Engulfed," by David D. Newsom, former Undersecretary of State for Political Affairs, 1978–81. *Foreign Policy* no. 43, Summer '81. p.17–32. Copyright © 1981 by Foreign Policy magazine. Reprinted by permission.

interests of the United States of America, and such an assault will be repelled by any means necessary, including military force."

President Reagan agrees. He has referred specifically to the need for U.S. ground forces in the region; a part of the defense budget increase aims to bolster U.S. capacity in the Indian Ocean; and the administration views the area as a key element in its global strategy.

When the Eisenhower Doctrine, which called for the United States to come to the aid of nations requesting assistance when attacked by countries "controlled by international communism," was promulgated in 1957, it was extensively debated in Congress and in the media. A joint resolution of Congress ultimately approved the doctrine.

The Carter Doctrine goes further. The United States now decides when to intervene, with or without a request. Despite this extension of U.S. discretion and responsibility, the American public has uncritically accepted the commitment to the Carter Doctrine, which itself grew out of last minute pressures for a presidential speech. There have been no congressional hearings and little public debate. As far as is known, neither the current administration nor the previous one has ever conducted a detailed study of the implications of the policy or its alternatives. The objective of a security framework for the Persian Gulf has quickly become part of accepted national policy.

Yet an intensive examination of the implications and practicality of this commitment, particularly the assumption that U.S. ground forces can and should be stationed in the area, is necessary. The recent history of the Middle East is littered with broken schemes for regional defense. Former Egyptian President Gamal Abdel Nasser killed the Middle East defense plan in 1954. The Iraqi revolution in 1958 undermined the Baghdad Pact. The Central Treaty Organization (CENTO) was a casualty of the Iranian revolution. U.S. national interest cannot afford more unpleasant shocks or regional disasters.

Any examination of U.S. security interests in the Persian Gulf must look at five critical questions: the nature of the threat; the attitudes in the area; the role of Western Europe; U.S. military capacity; and the possible alternative approaches. Any strategy must prevent the domination of the region by an unfriendly power and maintain the flow of oil. Both Carter and Reagan administration statements have emphasized the possibility of a military invasion by the Soviet Union. Whether Washington considers that threat imminent or distant will substantially affect the cost and form of the U.S. response. It will also determine the amount of pressure Washington should exert on others to cooperate.

Choke Points Against the USSR

A Soviet thrust into the area is neither as likely nor as feasible as current discussion would suggest. The Soviets have the military capacity to move into the Persian Gulf, and the invasion of Afghanistan brought their forces 800 miles closer to the area. Additional divisions across the Amu Dar'ya River and in Turkistan would intensify the threat. But the success of a Soviet invasion is not a foregone conclusion. A Pentagon official told the *New York Times* last year that even without opposition the Soviets would need five days to reach the gulf from Afghanistan. The 347 bridges, passes, and other vulnerable choke points on the way make the passage hazardous. General David Jones, chairman of the Joint Chiefs of Staff, warned Congress in February 1980 that "the Soviets clearly have the advantage of proximity. But it is a very difficult area. It isn't suitable for a blitzkrieg operation."

Moscow could also use its facilities in South Yemen and Ethiopia for such an operation, but hostile territory lies between those countries and the Soviet Union. The Soviet fleet in the Indian Ocean is inferior in numbers and power to its U.S. counterpart. In mid-1980 the USSR had 10 warships and 10 support ships in the area, whereas the U.S. fleet there consisted of 13 warships and six support ships, including two large carriers with 150 warplanes.

Soviet intentions are less clear. As part of their contingency planning, the Soviets have undoubtedly thought

through a military move against the Persian Gulf. Moscow
has signaled that it reserves the option to move forces into
Iran to counter any intervention there by rejecting Iranian
abrogation of the 1921 treaty between the two countries. Article VI declares:

In the case that there should be attempts from the part of a third
country to establish, through armed interference, an aggressive
policy on the territory of Persia and if the Government of Persia is
not strong enough to repel this danger, the government of the Soviet Union shall have the right to send its forces onto the territory
of Persia.

Russia has traditionally sought a warm-water port, although originally this policy was directed toward the Dar-
danelles. Some believe that the prospect of an energy shortage in the next two decades might lead the Soviets to seek
control over the Persian Gulf region. A less common view is
that the Soviets, in their desire for world domination, will attempt to control the Persian Gulf in order to extract political
concessions from Western Europe.

No current indications support these theories, and there is
no sign that the Soviets intend to move into the gulf any time
soon. Even with reinforcements, the Soviets have not committed the number of troops to Afghanistan that could
quickly end the revolt there. They are unlikely to move south,
leaving a strong insurgency along their border. Soviet naval
deployments in the Indian Ocean have remained at a more or
less constant level. Moscow's preoccupations remain China
and Eastern Europe, particularly Poland.

Although most observers expect the USSR to experience
an energy shortage in the near future, few anticipate one so
severe that the Soviets would risk the potentially catastrophic
military and political consequences of an attempt to seize the
gulf. In fact, the Soviets are seeking to export energy to Western Europe and Japan, not to import energy for their own use.

Despite the invasion of Afghanistan and Soviet propaganda efforts designed to prolong the U.S.–Iranian hostage
crisis, Moscow has not engaged in the kind of political activity in the gulf region that would precede an invasion. The So-

viets have suffered a setback in their hitherto close relations with Iraq. And they remain frustrated in revolutionary Iran, which suspended gas exports to the Soviet Union ostensibly because of a commercial dispute.

To both U.S. allies and the nations of the region, the Soviet threat is less imminent and real than the threat of political upheavals, with or without Soviet stimulation. What the U.S. response to such internal contingencies would be is less clear. Carter spoke of U.S. protection against "any outside force." Other American public figures have hinted that the United States would seize the oil fields rather than allow the West's energy life line to be endangered. Such statements are long remembered and inhibit cooperation with U.S. military plans.

U.S. military intervention to prevent or stop a conflict between states in the area or to support a friendly ruler in trouble would elicit broad-based opposition to the United States. Moreover, U.S. military intervention would very likely result in exactly what it sought to avoid: severely curtailed oil production. Political upheavals can, but need not, result in the loss of either production or access; outside intervention will almost certainly destroy both. Few believe that the United States could have prevented the outbreak of the Iran–Iraq war or that U.S. forces could have saved the shah. Countering internal threats to U.S. interests can be just as difficult as countering a Soviet military operation against the area.

Access to the Persian Gulf area cannot effectively be preserved without the cooperation of key states, particularly Turkey, Pakistan, Egypt, and Saudi Arabia. Turkey and Pakistan are the flanks that deter a Soviet move south. Egypt is the most practical major staging ground en route to the gulf. Without the use of Saudi territory, no strategy involving the use of U.S. forces to oppose an outside thrust into the gulf is workable. Iraq and Iran are also important, as major states in the area, but the prospect of early U.S. cooperation with either is remote.

Even in the case of Saudi Arabia, Pakistan, Turkey, and Egypt, formidable obstacles to full cooperation with the

United States remain. If Washington wishes to overcome those obstacles, it will have to be attentive to the nuances of Middle East politics. Thus, although all these countries will acknowledge their concern about the Soviet threat, they do so in part to gain leverage with the United States for their own immediate objectives. Iraq joined the Baghdad Pact in 1955, hoping to gain greater Western support for the Arab cause. Pakistan joined to strengthen itself against India. In 1978 Saudi Arabia evoked the Soviet threat to extract U.S. support for North Yemen; the Saudis, however, were keenly interested in gaining support for their own objectives there.

The Persian Gulf states welcome a U.S. military presence in the area, but they prefer it to be distant and unobtrusive. They believe that such a presence would provide security from both the Soviets and unpredictable neighbors. But the desire of local regimes for an outside presence is counterbalanced by fears that such a presence will increase their own political and military vulnerability.

The stationing of U.S. forces in the area would raise the most serious objections. Even nations that accepted the forces would carefully limit their mission. Turkey can tolerate foreign forces only as part of its obligations to the North Atlantic Treaty Organization (NATO). Oman, the one gulf state that has granted staging facilities to the United States, insists that the number of American forces be limited and confined to areas away from population centers. Egypt opposes the prolonged presence of U.S. forces except in a remote area of southern Egypt and refuses to sign a formal military facility agreement. Even if Cairo agrees to U.S. membership in a multilateral Sinai force to monitor the 1979 Egypt-Israel peace treaty, it is doubtful that the Egyptians will allow the troops to be equipped or available for other purposes. Most countries can justify foreign military personnel politically only if these forces equip and train domestic troops.

The aversion to foreign forces stems from many factors. Many believe such a presence increases their vulnerability to involvement in future wars. Troops are a reminder of the colonial past; they bring social and cultural problems. Traditional regimes know that the presence of foreign forces has been a successful rallying cry in revolutions. Nasser used the British presence along the Suez Canal to rally Egypt to his side. In Libya, the presence of America's Wheelus Air Force Base became an antimonarchy issue in the late 1960s. The shah of Iran suffered from internal opposition to the large American presence.

An American Balancing Act

Military relations between the United States and the regional states are also severely complicated by America's strong support for Israel. Arab unwillingness to cooperate results from a combination of deep resentment over Israeli occupation of East Jerusalem, which has religious as well as politial significance, and fear of Palestinian reprisals against anyone who deviates too far from the hard line on Palestinian issues. Palestinians constitute a strong minority in every gulf country, except Oman.

The Saudis, in particular, resent U.S. restrictions on the sale of military equipment because of the objections of Israel and its supporters in Congress. The latest problem that has arisen is the Saudi request for additional equipment that would increase the range and capability of U.S.-supplied F-15 aircraft and the U.S. offer to sell airborne warning and control system (AWACS) aircraft. Close U.S. cooperation with Saudi Arabia is essential to gulf defense. Yet the Reagan administration, like its predecessor, faces the difficult task of balancing the Saudi desire for advanced military equipment and the concerns of Israel for its security.

Many in the region doubt the constancy of U.S. policy. They wonder whether the United States will meet its commitments in critical situations and fear their security is subject to the whims of American public opinion. For example, Pakistan recalls that the United States cut off military assistance during the 1971 Indo-Pakistani war. Others consider the U.S. inability to find ways to support the shah of Iran against his domestic opponents as proof of American unreliability.

The fact that discussions and arrangements with the United States are often quickly made public also disturbs these countries. Even states experienced in dealing with the United States, such as Pakistan and Saudi Arabia, resent the inquiries of Congress into their internal affairs. Oman was embarrassed by the widespread publicity given to its cooperation with the United States during the hostage rescue mission in Iran.

Moreover, the difference between official and unofficial Western comment is not always understood in the Middle East. Conspiratorial views of the world lead many to believe that the unofficial may really represent the official. Unofficial statements by prominent figures out of government about seizing oil fields or using bases in the area in military contingencies are often confused with official declarations. When high government officials insist on airing their personal views even if those views do not agree with administration policy and when internal policy debate is allowed to spill over into public, the confusion only deepens. U.S. official statements of purpose must therefore be clear and consistent.

The greatest obstacle to good relations lies in what the United States asks and what it gives. States needing aid believe that U.S. responses are inadequate. They compare American offers with U.S. aid to others, particularly Israel and Egypt. In 1980 Pakistani President Mohammed Zia ul-Haq denounced a U.S. aid offer as "peanuts" and turned it down. The Pakistanis also resent the linking of U.S. security assistance to the closing down of their nuclear program. They see no U.S. response that would compensate for what they would consider a political and military loss.

The Reagan administration has reopened discussions with Pakistan. Although the new administration is very likely to be forthcoming, it will still face the problem of the Pakistani nuclear program, the ability of Pakistan to pay for arms purchases, and concern in Congress over the nature of the Zia regime.

Would a stronger American posture worldwide reduce the reluctance of these countries to cooperate with the United States? Would a more direct Soviet threat make these nations more receptive? Would a solution to the Palestine problem bring a dramatic change in attitudes?

These questions are hard to answer in the abstract. Ultimately, each Persian Gulf nation will decide what degree of cooperation with the United States is appropriate in terms of its own perception of its security and interests. The reluctance to allow a substantial U.S. military presence on land in this area has many causes. A change in one or more of these causes will not automatically open the door to unrestricted U.S. presence.

Susceptible Allies

The cooperation of Western Europe is essential to any American strategy for the Persian Gulf region. Western Europe is far more dependent on the region for its energy than is the United States, and consequently it has a greater stake in preserving access. France obtains 90 per cent of its petroleum from the Persian Gulf; Portugal, 80 per cent; Italy and Britain, 50 per cent; and West Germany, 35 per cent. Except in the case of Britain, where North Sea oil will reduce dependence, this situation is unlikely to change in the foreseeable future.

American forces can quickly reach the gulf region only through West European transit facilities and airspace. And Western Europe has the only outside military forces able to supplement U.S. capabilities in the region. Western Europe has, however, very different views on how to maintain access to the gulf.

As the West European reluctance to permit U.S. staging operations during the 1973 Arab-Israeli war demonstrated, transit rights are not assured. The most important and cooperative country is Portugal; its Lajes base in the Azores is vital. But even Portugal requests consultation on sensitive transits. All European allies will remain susceptible to Arab pressures not to cooperate with the United States on gulf issues. America's only assured transit rights in Western Europe are those relating to a NATO contingency, and the formal commitments of NATO members do not cover the gulf area.

France has the capacity to provide effective military support to the United States in the region. After the U.S. and Soviet fleets, the French fleet is the third largest in the Indian Ocean. French cooperation, however, is by no means certain. In the event of any major crisis, France's view of its interests, often different from the U.S. view, will guide its actions.

The United States could depend more on British help, but Britain's capacity is limited. It currently has five ships in the region. Japan also has a major stake in the gulf, but its constitutional limitations prevent it from sending any forces. Thus, its role will be limited to economic help to states such as Pakistan and Turkey.

Given their limited resources for deployment, the West European allies ought to make a greater effort in support of NATO. They would have to take up the slack should U.S. forces need to move from Western Europe to the Persian Gulf. So far, West European nations have been reluctant to face the political consequences of cutting back on domestic programs to finance a larger defense contribution. They hope that the United States will not need to redeploy NATO units during a gulf crisis; in the meantime, they are doing very little to prepare for such a possibility.

One solution would be to extend NATO responsibility formally to the Persian Gulf region. But this would encounter serious political opposition in Western Europe and in the gulf region itself. Even Turkey, the southern outpost of NATO, has been reluctant to discuss any involvement beyond its eastern borders.

Whereas the United States sees the problem of access to the gulf in strategic terms, West Europeans see it primarily in political terms. Concerned by the potential impact in Europe of an East-West confrontation in the gulf, they seek to preserve access by responding to the political and trade concerns of the nations in the gulf region. This is part of the motive for the West European Middle East initiative. Strong efforts to increase trade, including arms sales, to the states in the area reflect the economic needs of Western Europe as well as the belief that such activities will build a mutual interest protecting the concerns of both parties. Rather than risk a widened conflict, many West Europeans would acquiesce in a limited Soviet move in the area, such as a Soviet move into Azerbaijan in northwestern Iran, that did not touch the gulf itself.

These basic differences argue for close consultation between the United States and its European allies. But the question of how to consult is far from simple. The issue of defending the Persian Gulf would appear a normal subject for NATO consultations. Although members of the North Atlantic Council have raised the issue, the fear of leaks and the reaction of gulf countries inhibit many member states from discussing details in this forum. Moreover, France does not wish to appear to be included in NATO security discussions, a reluctance that also extends to expanded multilateral talks in any forum. The French attitude makes it difficult to include such significant countries as Japan, Italy, and Canada.

For the United States, meaningful consultation must be preceded by official discussions in Washington, including those with key members of Congress. The wider these discussions in Washington, the more authoritative will be the U.S. contribution to talks with others. Such discussions, however, inevitably run the risk that nations will learn of the U.S. plan in the media before consultations have begun overseas. This could lead to accusations of failure to consult, and make it more complicated for West European leaders to sell the policies to their own constituents. Consultations that genuinely seek to coordinate U.S. plans and objectives with those of other nations can, if taken seriously, also restrict the freedom of action of the United States, particularly on the sensitive Middle East question. Without an honest effort to consult, however, Washington cannot expect much allied support for U.S. initiatives in the region.

Starting from Scratch

When Carter declared his Persian Gulf doctrine, the United States had no capacity to back up that commitment with either troops or aircraft based in the region. Carter's statement was a formal expression of presidential intent, supporting the creation of a security framework yet to be formed. The framework was to consist of six parts: increased deployment of naval forces, particularly carrier forces, into the Indian Ocean; acquisition of access to facilities from friendly countries bordering on the Indian Ocean; use of rear basing facilities, primarily in Egypt; expansion of the existing U.S. base on the island of Diego Garcia; creation of a rapid deployment force; and increased military exercises in the area, particularly by Army and Marine ground units.

Except for the Indian Ocean fleet and the Diego Garcia base, the United States was starting from scratch in building Carter's security framework. Apart from a very limited air force presence in Zahran, Saudi Arabia, in the 1950s, the United States has never had a land-based military presence in or near the Persian Gulf region. Until recently, it did not even have a substantial regular fleet presence. Before 1971 gulf security rested on a limited British presence in the region. That presence began to diminish with Britain's departure from Egypt in 1954–1955 and was completed with its decision to withdraw naval and air forces from the Indian Ocean in 1970–1971.

U.S. military presence in the gulf area during this period consisted of two ancient seaplane tenders based on Bahrain. In subsequent years, this was augmented by two destroyers. Even today that force includes only five ships. Until 1979 U.S. naval deployments in the Indian Ocean consisted of periodic visits of task forces, including on occasion carrier task forces. With the revolution in Iran and the Soviet invasion of Afghanistan in 1979, two carrier task forces were assigned to the Indian Ocean. Their air power represented the only immediate American reaction force for Persian Gulf contingencies. These deployments stretched U.S. worldwide fleet capacity to the limit.

Even under the most favorable circumstances, American ability to move forces rapidly into the area is severely constrained. In December 1980 former National Security Adviser Zbigniew Brzezinski said that tactical air forces could be in the gulf region within hours, a battalion within 48 hours, and a division within two weeks. However, Pentagon planners said the division would take three weeks, assuming every available civilian transport plane were used.

At the least, it will be 1983 before the United States has the ability to lift two and one-half divisions—25,000 men—into the region. These could be augmented by tactical air squadrons and an additional carrier task force. The Soviets might bring to bear five times as much power. Even later in the decade, it is estimated that the maximum number of U.S. divisions available for rapid deployment will be six.

Because of limited air-lift capacity, the initial wave of these forces would have to depend on equipment, fuel, and water prepositioned in the area. The only assured prepositioning is currently at Diego Garcia, 2,500 miles from the gulf. The possibility exists that forces might have to join up with their equipment during a landing against hostile forces, a highly risky operation.

There are no other available facilities for forward base prepositioning of U.S. materiel in the event of combat. Backline basing rests on agreement with Egypt for the use of either Ras Banas or bases in the Sinai. The United States and Egypt do not currently have such an agreement. Facilities obtained in Kenya and Somalia are limited and far from the Persian Gulf. The availability of the facilities in Somalia could be affected by a conflict with Ethiopia.

Except for exercises conducted in Egypt by U.S. ground force units and in Kenya by Marines, Washington has been unable to arrange for such cooperation with other friendly countries in the area. The United States may face the prospect of deployment without any opportunity to become more familiar with the area and its features.

The build-up for effective deployment in the Persian Gulf area will be expensive. The ground force exercises conducted with 1,400 men in Egypt in 1981 cost about $25 million. The annual estimated costs in aid and military construction to gain access to facilities in the area exceed $5 billion. The actual equipment, including aircraft, will cost billions more.

The American people, suddenly conscious of the importance of the Persian Gulf, must consider several questions now. Will they continue their support as the vulnerability of the presence becomes more apparent? Would Congress agree to deployment in the face of an active threat, without a plan for extricating the force or giving it prompt additional support? Will the American public support so substantial an effort without a greater show of support by principal U.S. allies in Europe?

Other questions concerning the deployment of the force itself remain problematical. The circumstances in which the United States would commit forces to the gulf are undefined. Can Washington anticipate that gulf countries would request U.S. help? Would the United States move unilaterally? If so, would it encounter a hostile or friendly reception among the non-communist states?

Some observers note that Saudi Arabia called for American AWACS equipment following the outbreak of the Iran-Iraq war, arguing that Saudi Arabia would call in U.S. forces if it felt threatened. This is a risky extrapolation. The Saudis were responding to a specific threat within the region. Other gulf states did not oppose the request. The carefully confined presence of the aircraft does not raise the political and social questions that would be raised by an infusion of foreign ground forces.

Misinformation and Flimsy Analysis

Recognizing the Soviets' combat advantage in the area, the U.S. presence amounts to a trip wire. The Soviets would presumably be deterred by the prospect that an attack would risk direct contact with U.S. forces and the possibility of an escalation of conflict elsewhere. Is this a sufficiently valid basis for the substantial commitment of U.S. resources and the risk of deployment called for by this strategy? This escalation might result from a military confrontation in the area regardless of the U.S. posture. But as strategy, the threat has enormous and frightening implications because it is hard to envision such an escalation that does not culminate in a nuclear exchange. The West Europeans will not commit themselves to this approach if other alternatives are available. The United States should recognize that insuring access to the Persian Gulf opens a third theater for the U.S. military. It is not a case of rebuilding what once existed. It is a case of extending, at high cost, U.S. risk and responsibility.

Carter's statement of January 1980 established three objectives: to prevent the domination of the gulf region by an adversary; to block the further spread of Soviet influence; and to preserve access to oil for the industrial West. The President's statement and subsequent actions assumed full U.S. responsibility for the achievement of all these objectives. This strategy obviously faces numerous difficulties. Are there alternatives?

If one assumes that the primary deterrent to the Soviets is the risk of a direct encounter with U.S. forces, one possibility is to limit the presence and the possible response to U.S. naval and air forces in the region. This strategy would take advantage of the limited facilities already obtained in Oman, Somalia, and Kenya. It would avoid the greater difficulties involved in establishing a land-based U.S. presence in the area and would not disturb area states. If the Soviets were to strike, the U.S. fleet would itself be vulnerable to Soviet attack and serve as the trip wire.

Another alternative would concentrate on building the capacities of indigenous forces through arms sales and advisory aid. The United States already has arms sales and advisory programs in Saudi Arabia, Oman, and in peripheral states such as Egypt and Somalia. A strategy of supplying arms would encounter the opposition of other states in the region. Israel already strongly opposes sales to Saudi Arabia. India would object to an increased program of U.S. sales to Pakistan. The sentiments of Greece must always be taken into account in sales to Turkey. Furthermore, several of the states in the area would have problems effectively absorbing the sophisticated systems required to fight a determined Soviet thrust.

A further option would be a new regional defense arrangement involving the states of the area, the United States, and, possibly, interested West European countries. At the initiative of Kuwait, the Persian Gulf states are already considering a closer arrangement for economic as well as security consultations and coordination. However, few believe that this or any other arrangement could develop into the kind of Western-related regional defense structure that the Baghdad Pact and CENTO once attempted to be. Such concepts belong to the past.

Approaches have been suggested based on the integration of Israel into a regional defense arrangement or on the use of Israel to support U.S. deployments into the area. Clearly, under today's circumstances, any U.S. cooperation with Israel in a strategy involving the Arab states of the Persian Gulf would add enormous complications to an already complex problem. Israel is only slightly closer to the gulf than is Egypt. Using Israel instead of Egypt as a rear area base would have few advantages and many disadvantages.

An alternative popular in Western Europe urges the West to concentrate on insuring access to the gulf by building effective political ties with the area states. Sensitive responses to the arms needs of local states and to Palestinian demands, it is claimed, would secure good relations. A Western naval presence would not be excluded, but would be de-emphasized.

An agreement with the Soviets could also protect access to the area. In February 1981 the Soviets launched the idea of a conference with the West Europeans on assured access to the Persian Gulf. Soviet President Leonid Brezhnev repeated his proposal in more precise form during his visit to India and again during the recent Soviet party congress. Although tempting to some in Western Europe, the idea has gained little support. The Soviets would presumably require acceptance of their positions in Afghanistan, South Yemen, and Ethiopia as well as the reduction of the Western defense presence. The area states are equally unenthusiastic. Although reluctant to build up a conspicuous Western military presence, they nevertheless suspect the worst of the Soviets. The Arabs have no desire to invite the cat into the hen house.

According to strategic analysts Barry R. Posen and Steven W. Van Evera, "The new consensus behind large increases in the U.S. military budget coincides with a decline in the seriousness of the U.S. debate on security matters. The current public discussion of defense issues is ridden with misinformation and flimsy analysis." In no case is this more true than in the Persian Gulf debate.

Given existing doubts about the nature of the threat, the reception of an American presence in the area, the willingness of Western Europe to cooperate, and U.S. military capacity, a strategy that places U.S. ground forces in the Persian Gulf should not be undertaken without a thorough national and congressional debate. That debate has yet to begin.

In the meantime, the presence of America's substantial fleet should be maintained and its readiness strengthened. The United States should take maximum advantage of available facilities to support that presence. Allies and the states in the Persian Gulf area will accept such a posture. It will be consonant with a cold judgment of the current threat. It will provide a less expensive deterrent. It will meet the U.S. commitment to assure access to the area until such time as a genuine national debate decides that more is needed.

ARE OUR WEAPONS TOO COMPLEX?[6]

Under the spur of President Reagan, the Pentagon is galloping off on a spending spree which will total over $1 trillion between now and 1985, assuming peace prevails. War would cost more.

New planes, tanks, warships, submarines and missiles will be built as the Army, Navy, Air Force and Marine Corps all rush to modernize their arsenals depleted during the Vietnam War.

The question at the Pentagon is no longer whether President Carter's farewell fiscal 1982 defense budget, requesting a peacetime record of $196.4 billion, is enough, but how many billions should be added to it before Reagan sends his revised budget to Congress next month.

However, off to the side of this race to rearm stand some respected weapons specialists. They fear billions are being spent on the wrong kind of weapons, ones too complicated to depend on in a muddy battle far from any defense contractor's repair depot. If their fears are justified, soldiers may pay with their lives for faulty weapons.

"A tank hatch that a soldier, clothed for winter, cannot fit through; a major shipboard fire control system that cannot be adequately supported; aircraft test equipment that causes more problems than it solves, and a hand-held missile that when fired startles the person that fires it, resulting in misses, are some examples of the problems with currently fielded weapon systems," complained the General Accounting Office after studying what the Pentagon is buying.

"The demand for high performance has forced designers to incorporate new technology into systems often before its

[6] Reprint of two newspaper articles, "Are Our Weapons Too Complex?" by George C. Wilson, Pentagon reporter, and "Not If You Compare Them to the Russians'," an interview conducted by Wilson with William J. Perry, Undersecretary of Defense for Research and Engineering during the Carter administration. *The Washington Post,* C1+. F. 22, '81. Copyright © 1981, The Washington Post. Reprinted by permission.

reliability has been fully assessed," scolded the GAO in accusing the Pentagon of buying overly fancy weapons. This is the perennial "goldplating" charge.

Zeroing in on specific weapons in its recent report entitled, "Effectiveness of U.S. Forces Can Be Increased Through Improved Weapon System Design," the congressional watchdog agency leveled these criticisms at the Pentagon's supposed technological wonders:

—Air Force F15 fighter. The Pentagon demanded too much from the plane's Pratt & Whitney F100 engine, causing it to break down frequently, and bought repair equipment for the F15 that is unreliable. "Without modification," GAO said of the flawed test equipment, "it seems doubtful" that the readiness of F15s to go to war can be improved adequately.

—Army Cobra helicopter TOW missile launcher. It breaks down every 100 hours, meaning the helicopter cannot be counted on to destroy enemy tanks over an extended period.

—Navy Mk-86 fire control system. "When the system is inoperable, the ship is virtually defenseless." Yet in 1979, the firing system was in working order only about 60 percent of the time as one after another of its 40,000-plus parts failed. "Also, there is a long learning curve for repair technicians because of the system's complexity."

—Army M60A2 tank. "The tank has a long history of unreliability." Its turret is "fantastically complex," according to an Army unit commander quoted by the GAO. Although the GAO did not discuss the Army's new XM1 main battle tank, which costs $1.6 million each, it, too, has been criticized as overly complicated.

Except for the M60 tank, which is being replaced by the XM1, the Reagan administration plans to buy more of those same weapons as Defense Secretary Caspar Weinberger carries out his mission "to rearm America."

Other alarms are being sounded within the Pentagon itself. Franklin C. Spinney, a tactical air warfare specialist in the Pentagon's program analysis office, contends in a report,

"Defense Facts of Life," that the Pentagon often buys technology for technology's sake, not for the difference it would make in battle.

"Although we buy technology to support soldiers in war," complains Spinney in his report, which Sen. Sam Nunn of Georgia hailed as a breakthrough in frankness, "plans and decisions do not use the criteria of actual combat to evaluate the potential contributions of emerging technology.

"Technology is evaluated within an artificial framework derived from the faith in technological revolution, the attrition mind-set and the idea that war is a manipulable, deterministic process subject to central control. This framework considers neither the decisive effect of the human elements nor the central characteristic of actual war . . . There is no senior Pentagon staff organization chartered to study war, particularly how soldiers act in war and how we can use emerging technology to make these actions more effective."

"Although the study of history can be carried too far," Spinney continues, "history is the only evidence of real war. And to ignore it completely leads to a modern form of medieval scholasticism: the religion of miracle weapons. Hitler provides an ominous precedent for this unrealistic faith in technology, an observation suggesting a disturbing question: Was Hitler's faith in miracle weapons apparent between 1939 and 1941 when he was winning, or was it apparent in 1944 and 1945 when he was losing?"

"By ignoring the real world," Spinney warns, "we have evolved a self-reinforcing, yet scientifically unsupportable, faith in the military usefulness of ever increasing technological complexity. We tend to think of military strength in terms of wonder weapons that are in reality mechanistic solutions . . .

"The costs of increasing complexity can be generalized into low readiness, slower modernization and declining forces" as the wonder weapons become so expensive that only a few can be bought at a time, and those few are hard to keep in working order. "The crucial question is: Are there positive qualities of complexity to outweigh these negative qualities?"

Spinney answers his own question in the negative, declaring: "The across-the-board thrust towards ever-increasing technological complexity just is not working. We need to change the way we do business . . . Our strategy of pursuing ever increasing technical complexity and sophistication has made high technology solutions and combat readiness mutually exclusive."

NOT IF YOU COMPARE THEM TO THE RUSSIANS'

For the past four years, William J. Perry has been Mr. Technology at the Pentagon. He was the undersecretary of defense who supervised the development and purchase of these wonder weapons that the critics are now faulting. In two lengthy interviews with *The Washington Post,* Perry, who has been retained by the Reagan administration temporarily as a consultant, defended the course he took. Here is what he said:

Q: Are the weapons the Pentagon is buying too complicated for the realities of battle?

A: Another way to put that question is: Wouldn't it be better, simpler, less complicated to go back to P51 airplanes [of World War II]? Go back to guns instead of missiles? The only trouble with that argument is that it overlooks the competition. If we could persuade the Soviets to go back with us, that wouldn't be a bad idea.

Unfortunately, Soviet tactical aircraft generally are more complex, more sophisticated than ours. The claim that they are simpler and more reliable is nonsense. People who make that claim are thinking about the Mig19 and Mig21. They are simple, reliable airplanes. But the Mig23, Mig25 and Mig27 that the Soviets have built in the last decade are, in general, more complex, more expensive than comparable U.S. airplanes.

Our trend has been toward simplifying technological complexity. Their trend has been in exactly the opposite direction. We have changed roles. All of their modern tactical fighter airplanes are variable geometry wings [meaning they can be swept back along the fuselage for high-speed flight and extended straight out for takeoff and landing]. Now talk about something which makes an airplane complex and expensive—that's it. That goes back to our F111 [TFX, built under former defense secretary Robert S. McNamara]. Their tactical airplanes are somewhat smaller versions of F111s, whereas we deliberately moved away from variable sweep wings on the F15, F16 and F18 to avoid that complexity.

Q: Air Force leaders have conceded that they overreached in setting down requirements for the F15's F100 engine. Isn't that a documented case of buying an overly complicated weapon?

A: I have mixed feelings about the F15. I think we overreached on the specifications for the engine when we designed it by pushing for that last 10 percent of performance. And we got it. But we paid a heavy price for it in terms of cost, reliability and maintainability of the engine. That's a problem we will fix and are fixing. I truly believe the Air Force's assertion that the F15 is the best fighter airplane in the world. Part of the reason for the F15's superiority, by no means the whole reason, is the performance of that engine.

Q: Do you think it's also a myth that Soviet tanks are simpler and more reliable than our tanks?

A: The Soviet T64, which is the high-technology Russian tank, is as complex as any tank we have built in terms of the gadgets that are on it: the night vision devices, the laser systems, the computer control firing systems. Also it has an automatic loading system, which ours does not. We still think our XM1 will outperform the T64 or any other Soviet tank.

If you really start to describe the complexity in weapons systems, and then you compare the current Soviet systems toe-to-toe with current U.S. systems, generally theirs are more complex.

Look what the Soviets are doing with their navy now. They built the largest, most complex cruiser in the world; they built the largest submarine in the world [the nuclear-powered Typhoon missile submarine]. They built the largest cruise missile submarine in the world, the Oscar. The U.S. Trident missile submarine is a simpler, cheaper system than the Typhoon. And certainly our 688 attack class submarines, which are capable of carrying as many cruise missiles as the Oscar, are simpler and cheaper.

Q: Haven't our new wonder weapons become too complicated for the ordinary soldier in the field to operate?

A: There is tremendous confusion on this point because people equate complexity with technology. A hand-operated calculator is a very, very sophisticated piece of technology. But if you compare the ease of operation and the ease of maintainability of that with the electromechanical desk calculators that were around five or 10 years ago, you realize that we've taken a giant step forward in simplicity.

The reason our equipment in the field today is hard to operate and hard to maintain is that most of it is 15 to 20 years old and loaded with electromechanical devices long past their useful life. They were never very easy to operate and maintain in the first place. But we're replacing that junk with new generations of weapons that are more reliable and much easier to operate and maintain.

If you compare the new XM1 tank with tanks we drove in World War II, you'll find it's much easier to drive the XM1. I could teach you to drive an XM1 tank and fire its gun in five minutes. And you would have a fair chance of hitting a moving target a mile away while you're moving with your first shot. You see a tank on a screen and then have to do two things: move a cursor [a dot of light] to put a little bull's eye on the target and pull the trigger twice. The first time the trigger sends out a laser beam to measure the distance to the enemy tank. A fraction of a second later you pull the second trigger and that shoots the gun. Between the time of pressing the first and second triggers the computer in the tank has decided how the gun should be pointed, and points it. And the computer is continuously sampling sensors to determine windage and tank motion. All this is happening in the computer. All you do is pull the two triggers.

I think the XM1 tank is the best in the world. It's superior to anything we've ever had and anything the Soviets have—across the board in performance, reliability, ease of operation and maintenance. Tremendous emphasis was put during the design stage to provide reliability and ease of maintenance. One way you get this is by substituting microelectronics—integrated circuits, for example—for electromechanical devices.

I think the XM1 tank is better than the T64 or T72. But our XM1s are still in our factories while their T72s are out in the field. It'll be a couple of years before we have enough XM1s deployed to make a difference.

Q: How about strategic weaponry: Are Soviet intercontinental ballistic missiles [ICBMs] bigger but less complicated and more reliable than ours?

A: Soviet missiles today are not simple. They are still big, but they are no longer simple. The Soviet ICBMs are much bigger than their U.S. counterparts, and they are also liquid fueled instead of solid fueled. They are less efficient than their American counterparts. The new Soviet ICBMs, unlike the ones of the 1960s, have very complex guidance systems run by three independent computers.

As a consequence, the Soviet SS18 and SS19 ICBMs have accuracies comparable to U.S. ICBMs. That's a distinction between the ICBMs of the 1960s and the 1970s. So, while they have remained large and relatively inefficient in terms of nuclear yield per ton of missile, they are no longer simple and they are no longer inaccurate.

Q: If we are indeed more efficient, getting more bang for the buck, why are there so many alarms coming from the Pentagon about new Soviet weapons?

A: As I'm all too agonizingly aware, from the time you actually spend research and development money until the time the money is converted to deployed military capability is a good many years. Therefore, the fact that the Soviets have been ahead of us in defense research and development spending for a decade doesn't give them an instant capability. But we are beginning to see now the fruits of that extra spending.

Things which 10 years ago we could sit back and say, "Well, we're comfortably ahead of them": ICBM guidance; look-down-shoot-down missiles and radars; submarine detection systems—we could tick off these great advantages we had over the Soviets which made a whale of a difference. These advantages allowed us to say the large size of the Soviet systems is not a matter of great concern.

Now the cumulative effect of the Soviets' spending more for the last 10 years on military research and development than the United States is beginning to be felt, beginning to be observed in deployed systems. We now see a deployed Soviet ICBM with guidance comparable to our guidance; we now see look-down, shoot-down missile and radar in the final test stage, which we expect to be deployed soon, which in some ways is comparable to the capability we have.

So, to a certain extent, the difference is that they were behind, and it has taken them a while to catch up. There is another fundamental difference, though, which is going to be true on into the 1980s. That is that their research and development program is less efficient than ours, fundamentally because they don't have the high technology commercial industry to base it on.

Our great advantage in defense is in microelectronics, microcomputers, which have been based on the advances conceived, sponsored and paid for by commercial research and development to a very considerable extent. The Soviets don't have anything comparable. So, simply comparing U.S. and Soviet military research and development budgets does not tell the whole story.

EDITOR'S INTRODUCTION

During the last few years a new political consensus has formed in support of increased defense spending. Ronald Reagan was elected to the Presidency at least in part because of his commitment to raise military expenditure. He promised a reversal of national priorities, proposing to compensate for a surge in defense spending with corresponding cuts in social programs.

Nonetheless, many economists and congressmen, including staunch advocates of military strength, expressed fears about the long-term effects of defense spending on the federal deficit and inflation. Robert G. Kaiser of the *Washington Post* details these concerns in this section's first article. The staff of the *Economist* offers a rebuttal in the second.

For the fiscal year 1982, the Reagan administration got almost all the defense dollars it wanted. A debate continues, however, as to whether the military's spending emphasis should be on nuclear weapons, conventional arms, or improved salaries and readiness. Donald D. Holt of FORTUNE magazine offers an assessment of the Carter and the Reagan five-year defense spending programs for the period 1982–86. FORTUNE's own defense spending recommendations fall somewhere between the two proposals. In this section's fourth article, Gene R. LaRocque strongly criticizes the Reagan administration's spending priorities.

A budget decision is not, however, the final word on defense; raising military spending will not ensure national security. A new school of military reformers, whose adherents include Edward N. Luttwak and U.S. Senator Gary Hart, offer wide-ranging criticism of prevailing concepts of U.S. military strategy, weaponry and officer training. Luttwak is a self-proclaimed hawk; Hart was formerly manager of George McGovern's unsuccessful presidential campaign. Although their political views are opposed, their criticisms of the current U.S. military establishment are surprisingly consistent. They ask not only whether we are spending enough on defense, but whether we are asking ourselves the right questions about America's defense in the 1980s.

REAGAN'S DEFENSE SPENDING COULD TURN INTO ECONOMIC NIGHTMARE[1]

There is a potential Republican nightmare for 1984 buried in the Reagan administration's "Program for Economic Recovery." It can be found under "D"—for defense.

If Congress enacts the enormous Reagan defense program, as it now seems eager to do, and if the national economy fails to perform as well as the administration predicts it will, that nightmare could become reality. If a tax cut is passed and the promised Reagan boom fails to materialize, what is supposed to be a balanced budget in 1984 could have a $50 billion to $100 billion deficit.

Every major economic forecasting firm and the Congressional Budget Office say that the boom won't materialize.

The significance of the administration's proposals can be stated in simple numbers. This year the Pentagon will spend about $103 billion. By 1984, according to the administration's optimistic calculation, that figure will rise to $256 billion. By the Congressional Budget Office's reckoning (the CBO is more pessimistic than the administration's Office of Management and Budget about the prospects for reducing inflation), the 1984 figure actually will be $267 billion, or a 64 percent increase in just three years.

Commentary

Stated another way, the Reagan administration proposes to *increase* defense spending in the next three years by an amount greater than the entire defense budget of 1978. In

[1] Reprinted from a newspaper article "Reagan's Defense Spending Could Turn Into Economic Nightmare," by Robert G. Kaiser, staff writer. *Washington Post.* p.1+. Ap. 25, '81. Copyright © 1981, The Washington Post. Reprinted by permission.

constant dollars this buildup would be three times larger than the Vietnam war buildup—and it was that late-1960s strain on the economy, numerous economists say, that provoked America's current economic problems.

Conditions have changed since the late '60s, and there are economists who believe that the economy and the federal budget can absorb the huge defense increases that President Reagan favors (in real terms, an 11.5 percent increase in budget authority this year, a 14.8 percent increase next year). Several administration economists pointed out that even if the Reagan buildup is fully approved by Congress, defense spending will represent a smaller portion of GNP than it did in the late '60s—about 7 percent compared to 10 percent then. But the proposed increases are unprecedented in size and there is great political momentum now behind them, a combination that makes this potential nightmare at least worth considering.

Few politicians in Washington seem to be considering it just yet. Congress is rushing into the new defense program with unanimity and, thus far, very little scrutiny.

Theoretically, nothing would prevent the administration from cutting back on defense spending if it saw the economy falling behind its optimistic predictions. Lawrence Kudlow, chief economist at the Office of Management and Budget, made this point in an interview, saying: "If any overall budgetary adjustments are necessary [in the future], then they'll be made. . . . Defense expenditures are always considered as part of the overall budget picture."

But defense spending is not so easy to alter, particularly in the midst of a multiyear buildup like the one now beginning. For example, if the Reagan administration were to decide in January 1983 that excessive defense spending jeopardized any chance at a balanced budget in 1984, it would find that it had already lost control of all but about 16 percent of the procurement outlays scheduled for the 1984 defense budget.

This is because money appropriated for defense programs in one year actually is spent over the next several years. According to figures compiled by the CBO, $72 billion will be spent on procurement of weapons and equipment in 1984 under the Reagan budget. But in January 1983, $61 billion of that amount already would be appropriated (most of it in the '82 and '83 budgets), so it would be locked in and beyond the reach of any sudden effort to cut defense spending. Only about $11 billion of the '84 outlays would remain to be appropriated after January 1983.

The nonprocurement sections of the budget would be equally hard to reduce suddenly, because they represent money spent to support and maintain forces in being.

Moreover, defense spending is more than just another item in the Reagan budget. The new administration has made a stronger national defense its top spending priority, and has treated funds for the Pentagon as a unique budget category. While the Office of Management and Budget has been slicing away at almost every department in the government, the Reagan White House actually gave the Pentagon more than it asked for in its 1982 budget.

According to sources inside OMB, the usual staff work was dispensed with this winter as the new administration rushed to pump more dollars into defense.

The administration has further committed itself to huge defense outlays by promising to stick to the program it has outlined, even if its price goes up. Defense Secretary Caspar W. Weinberger has testified at least twice that if inflation pushes up costs, he'll return to Congress to ask for more money.

That prospect raises fears among some economists of a repetition of the Vietnam experience. Lyndon B. Johnson refused to raise taxes to pay for his Vietnam buildup, insisting that the Great Society could have both guns and butter. Instead, he set off the inflation that still plagues the United States.

Now President Reagan proposes a much bigger buildup in absolute terms, and one that is just as big as a percentage of current gross national product.

Not all economists agree that the defense buildup Reagan proposes is inherently dangerous. Some economists believe the economy now has enough slack to cope with this buildup relatively easily, perhaps at the cost of about an additional one percent added to the inflation rate. That was the consensus among several of the nation's best-known economic forecasters at a Pentagon-sponsored seminar last fall.

But those economists all assumed that a big military buildup would be financed either by a tax increase or by cuts in other forms of government spending. The Reagan budget proposes to balance increased defense spending with a new boom in the domestic economy.

As calculated by Prof. Lester C. Thurow of the Massachusetts Institute of Technology (an adviser to Democratic politicians who is unabashedly critical of the Reagan program), Reagan proposes to offset a $196 billion tax cut and a $181 billion increase in defense spending with $138 billion in civilian spending cuts. Then new revenue generated by vigorous economic growth hypothetically would balance the Reagan budget by 1984.

Thurow is one of the economists who has argued that the Reagan defense progam could create serious new economic difficulties. Another is Wassily Leontief, Nobel Prize-winning economist now at New York University, who said in a recent interview: "If handled improperly, these huge jumps in military spending will mean higher inflation, a worsening balance-of-payments gap, a drain on productive investment, soaring interest rates, increasing taxes, a debased currency and, in the longer term, more unemployment."

Leontief disputes the administration's optimism.

"Reagan hopes our gross national product will expand so much that we will be able to pay for higher defense spending without raising taxes," he told *U.S. News and World Report.* "This is not likely to happen. In fact, I personally guarantee that it will not happen."

Administration economists argue otherwise. Kudlow of OMB contends that the administration's budgetary and monetary policies will bring down the inflation rate, thus in effect holding down the real cost of defense spending. He disputed any suggestion that high defense spending might itself aggravate inflation.

"We've done a study on that," Kudlow said. It concluded that when defense spending was high in the 1960s, inflation was low, he said, but when defense spending fell dramatically as a percentage of GNP in the '70s, inflation rates soared.

There are numerous unanswered questions about the potential economic impact of the Reagan defense budget, but few of them have yet been raised in any congressional committee or other official forum.

First of all, the simple budgetary facts have been obscured, largely by rhetoric about the president's "budget-cutting" crusade. In fact, Reagan is not proposing to cut the federal budget. He is proposing to slow the rate at which it will grow. Instead of reducing the budget, the administration wants to transfer billions previously earmarked for social programs into defense.

If the Reagan budget were adopted by Congress, and OMB's optimistic forecasts for the economy came true, this is what would happen to the federal budget and the national economy:

Gross national product would grow 41 percent, from $2.9 trillion in 1981 to $4.1 trillion in 1984. Civilian expenditures in the federal budget would grow from $493.1 billion to $614.6 billion, a 25 percent increase. And outlays for defense would rise 60 percent from $162 billion to $260 billion in 1984—and continue growing to $343 billion in 1986. (All of these figures are in current dollars, unadjusted for inflation.)

Using the CBO's less optimistic economic assumptions, the 1984 defense budget might be 10 percent higher than Reagan predicts. But the CBO also believes that the administration underestimates the rate at which the prices of defense-related goods are rising. To complete the programs in the Reagan budget could cost $50 billion more by 1984 than the administration expects, CBO has estimated.

Defense-sector inflation is another area that has received almost no public attention in the discussion so far over Reagan's defense proposals. In fact, prices for military goods are rising 50 percent faster than the underlying rate of inflation.

Some weapons systems have more than doubled in cost just in the last two years. The unit cost of the Army's new, advanced armored personnel carrier, for example, rose 94.8 percent in 1979 and another 65 percent in 1980. A modified version of the C130 air transport equipped with advanced electronics went up in price 75.9 percent in 1979 and another 26 percent last year. The price of an F18 jet fighter, in which the Reagan administration plans to invest heavily, went up 25 percent in 1979 and 44 percent in 1980.

Overall, the costs of the 47 major weapons systems now being purchased by the Pentagon rose more than 20 percent in 1980. According to a CBO calculation, while the underlying rate of inflation in the economy as a whole last year was 9.3 percent, costs of defense purchases went up 14.9 percent. For four years up to 1980, the same index shows, defense-sector inflation was less than a point higher than inflation generally; the sudden jump last year hints at a new explosion in defense costs.

This is another area that has received relatively little public attention, although a number of gloomy (and prolix) official reports have been written on the subject. During the 1970s, when defense spending fell to the lowest levels (as a percentage of GNP) of the postwar era, what has been called the military-industrial complex changed radically. Thousands of small firms that were subcontractors to the giant defense firms in the 1960s—providing 50 to 60 percent of the components of most major weapons systems—went out of business, or out of the defense business.

In many critical areas, there are only one or two firms in the United States that can provide key parts. According to the Pentagon's Defense Science Board, only two companies make the titanium wing skins crucial to advanced aircraft; only three firms make aircraft landing gear; just one manufactures special ball bearings for air frames. Only two shipyards in the country—both of them already working at full capacity—can build many of the ships in the new Navy budget.

As a result of real or potential bottlenecks such as these, the waiting times for the Pentagon to take delivery on major weapons systems after they are ordered have stretched into years. According to the Defense Science Board, the waiting time for an F15 jet fighter is 41 months; for an A10, 49 months. Numerous experts have testified that the U.S. defense industry does not have the capacity to sustain a surge in production to meet the needs, for example, of an unexpected military conflict, and the surge called for in the Reagan budget will be difficult to satisfy.

Bottlenecks in domestic defense industries and a sudden intensification of defense orders contribute to another little-discussed repercussion from a new defense buildup: the stimulation of an increase in imports. Last fall, the major economic forecasters met in a seminar sponsored by the Pentagon to discuss the possible impact of a surge in defense spending. Although they all differed in their predictions, all agreed that increased imports would be one consequence.

Thurow of MIT argues that a defense buildup could prove more profitable to West Germany and Japan than to the United States, partly because of the new sales it will mean for firms in that country, partly because American defense industries draw off the best engineers and skilled labor.

"Would you rather work on designing a new missile with a laser guidance system, or on designing a new toaster?" Thurow has written. "To ask the question is to answer it. Military research and development is more exciting. . . . The military is willing to pay almost any premium to have a better product. The civilian economy is not. As a result, the very best brains move into defense."

"If the skilled personnel and funds that are used for defense here are used for civilian production abroad," Thurow added, "it should not come as a great surprise when we are driven out of civilian markets. What happens to us if we are driven out of semiconductors, microprocessors and computers while we are busy rearming ourselves?"

None of these questions about the potential impact of the Reagan defense program have been raised very loudly in Congress. Critics can be found, particularly on the liberal end of the political spectrum, but few of them volunteer their views before they are solicited.

"You're going to spend more, get less, and ultimately put yourself in a far more dangerous position," according to Rep. Thomas J. Downey (D-N.Y.). Downey, a member of the House Budget Committee, then was asked if he would try to delete any of the defense program from the budget resolution. No, he said. "It's no use."

THE $176 BILLION QUESTION[2]

Last year Americans voted that they were rightly worried about their safety. By some time in the early 1980s Russia's new intercontinental ballistic missiles will probably be able to destroy America's entire land-based nuclear missile force in a single cataclysmic attack. This challenge to the central nuclear power of the United States is being added to the Warsaw pact's long-time superiority in conventional forces, at a time when Russia is adopting a more aggressive political posture all round the world.

Because of these fears, defence spending has been hurriedly increased by President Carter. During the Carter years real defence spending rose by an average of 2.6% a year, bunched towards the end of his administration. In the election Mr Carter promised a real rise in defence spending of 5% a year for 1981–84, and he presented figures for this in his parting budget last January.

Mr Reagan then had a problem. Having made so much of his predecessor's weak defence record, it would not do simply to endorse his increases. Mr Reagan felt he had to promise to

[2] Reprint of a magazine article, "The $176 billion question," by the staff of *The Economist.* pp. 15–8. S. 12, '81. Copyright © 1981 by The Economist. Reprinted by permission.

What Mr Reagan planned to do for defence

Total obligational authority	1981	1982	1983	1984	1985	1986
			($billion)			
Current prices	178.0	222.2	253.8	288.2	325.5	366.5
Constant Fy (1982) prices	193.9	222.2	238.4	255.1	272.9	292.0
% increase over previous year (constant $)	12.4	14.6	7.3	7.0	7.0	7.0
% increase over Carter plan for same year (constant $)	4.0	13.1	15.6	17.8	20.0	22.3
Outlays						
Total current prices	158.6	184.8	220.4	249.1	296.6	335.3
Total constant Fy (1982) prices	174.0	184.8	205.6	218.1	245.3	263.3
% increase over previous year (constant $)	7.0	6.2	11.3	6.1	12.5	7.3
% increase over Carter plan for same year (constant $)	0.9	2.7	9.2	10.7	18.5	21.1
Assumed inflation (gnp deflator)	—	8.4%	7.0%	6.4%	5.4%	5.0%

spend more still. So a re-worked defence budget was quickly produced in March, promising a 14.6% real increase in "total obligational authority" in fiscal 1982 (which starts in October) and then an average 7%-per-annum real rise in fiscal 1983 through 1986 (see table).

Most of the large 1982 rise is for a crash programme to improve America's military readiness, which the Reagan team rightly judged to be in a sorry state. It includes such specific items as rebuilding run-down stocks of ammunition and spare parts, better pay to attract more and better soldiers, repairing some of the long backlog in maintenance and modernisation. This 1982 increase is thus being allocated to meet known needs.

The rest of the five-year plan has no such logic behind it. The figure of 7% per annum average real increase was chosen, not out of consideration for any military imperatives, but because the figure was 2% more than Mr Carter's.

The Reagan defence plan involves some pretty staggering increases. In nominal terms, defence spending is projected to rise from $158.6 billion in 1981 to $249 billion by the time Mr Reagan is up for re-election in 1984, and then to $335 billion by 1986. This last figure is higher than the entire gnp of Britain down to three years ago. To reach it America will have to institute a $176 billion rise in defence spending over five years, and hoist the proportion of the federal budget going to defence from 24% now to 38% then (partly because non-defence spending will be held down by painful cuts in social services).

It is this projected rise of $176 billion which Mr David Stockman, the budget director, is anxious to pare down by $30 billion or so. He wants to make the biggest cuts in fiscal 1983 and 1984, so that Mr Reagan will have a chance of reaching his promised balanced budget in 1984. Since the total rise is based on a 7%-a-year real increase which was conjured up mainly to outspend Mr Carter, there is every reason to scrutinise it with the same parsimony that Mr Stockman brings to food stamp programmes and training schemes for unemployed blacks. But before recommending where it might be scaled back without delighting the Russians, the $176 billion rise needs to be placed in perspective, for it has been the subject of much misrepresentation.

Defence and Nonsense

A main source of such misunderstanding was an article by Professor Lester Thurow in the May 14th *New York Review of Books*, entitled "How to wreck the economy". Professor Thurow, a former adviser to presidential candidate George McGovern and now of the Massachusetts Institute of Technology, is one of the best liberal economists around. His recent book, "Zero-Sum Society", is full of sound sense. But on defence he trumpeted to varied liberals and conservatives that "the military build-up currently being contemplated is three times as large as the one that took place during the Vietnam war". This is a matter that can be decided by the facts, and the facts are not with Mr Thurow.

The Vietnam build-up was concentrated between 1965 and 1968, when real defence spending shot up by 47%. Between 1981 and 1984 Mr Reagan envisages real defence outlays to increase by 25%—or just a little over half the defence increase of the Vietnam peak years, when the real inflationary damage was done because President Johnson was also spending heavily on creating a Great Society (which President Reagan certainly will not be). During the full five years of the Reagan programme real defence outlays are projected to rise by 51%, which is a little more than the Vietnam build-up (though hardly three times). But Reagan rearmament will be spread over five years, with an average growth in outlays of 10%; peak Vietnam spending rose by 16% a year, crammed into only three years.

In terms of its share of the nation's resources, the Reagan rearmament is the smallest of the three major build-ups since 1945. During the Vietnam war, defence spending rose to 9% of the gross national product. During the Korean war it peaked at 13.3%. The Reagan plan is estimated to add only 0.3% a year to defence's share of the gnp, which means it will reach 7.1% of gnp by 1986 if Mr Reagan's forecasts for gnp prove right (which they admittedly won't).

There is one sense, however, in which the Vietnam years are instructive. President Johnson refused to raise taxes to pay for an unpopular war and America soon reaped an inflationary whirlwind. Mr Reagan is offering guns and butter too. Over the next five years he is proposing $750 billion of tax cuts and $176 billion of extra defence spending—matched, so far, by only $130 billion of budget cuts. The tax cuts have ballooned because income tax is supposed to be index-linked to inflation in the later years. Conjecture beyond 1984 helps nobody, but Mr Stockman's present focus is on the next three years.

Mr Stockman has told the president that a balanced budget by 1984 will require an extra $74 billion in cuts ($30 billion from the 1983 budget, $44 billion from 1984). He wants defence to contribute $30 billion of this $74 billion. He is probably too optimistic in thinking that even $74 billion of cuts will bring balance, but too conservative in saying that balance is needed.

The prediction of a 1984 balanced budget was based on the workings of a supply-side miracle, bringing high growth (over 4% per year increase in real gnp) and low inflation (around 5% a year). With an economy growing flat out at 4% a year, the model rightly said that America would have inflation far above an annual 5% if the administration planned for large budget deficits.

In practice, however, America is not going to get 4% annual growth. In a slack economy budget deficits need not be inflationary. The deficit for fiscal 1982 will probably be well over the proposed $42.5 billion. But even if it rises to $60 billion (which is likely), that will still be less than 2% of gnp, which will edge over an annual $3 trillion at the end of 1981.

Still, the bigger the cut, the better for Mr Reagan's economic strategy. Where can the defence part of the axe fall without endangering America's military security?

The Strategic Choices

America's three armed services are particularly skilled at fighting each other for money. As soon as Mr Reagan's defence team moved into the Pentagon all three began manoeuvring not only to proceed with most of the programmes they had been left with (which would themselves have used up most of the 7% annual increases), but also to add a lot of new ones. Each service trotted out a list of pet projects as if it expected to have the entire 7% to itself. Even without Mr Stockman's looming axe, Mr. Caspar Weinberger would have had to make enemies of some top brass. He needs to make hard choices.

The most urgent task is to strengthen America's vulnerable strategic forces. Top priority should go to the new MX intercontinental ballistic missile (ICBM), and to basing it in some way so that it will be invulnerable to a Russian first strike. The development of the MX missile itself is well under way, but both the Reagan and Carter administrations have been puzzled where to place it and how to protect it. All the best schemes are expensive, and involve much spending before 1984.

The Carter administration's "loading dock" scheme for shuttling 200 MXes between 4,600 horizontal shelters in Utah and Nevada would have cost over $30 billion at 1980 prices. A curious combination of environmentalists and right-wingers seems to have killed that. Mr Weinberger's problem is that none of the dozens of options he has reviewed is militarily much better or cheaper.

His best course would be to plump for a scaled-down version of the Carter loading-dock scheme: to disperse perhaps 100 missiles among 1,000 shelters in those counties in Nevada which have offered to take them. It is important to proceed quickly with a survivable ICBM programme and slam shut the "window of vulnerability"—the time during which Russia might be tempted to strike first in the belief that it could knock out all America's land-based missiles. Nearly $3 billion is already allocated to MX development in the 1982 budget.

A system that could survive a first strike could be in place by 1986.

The weakness of such a scaled-down MX basing system is that it might not close the window of vulnerability for very long. Either it would eventually have to be expanded to something approaching its original 4,600-shelter plan as the Russians trained more warheads on to it. Or some other protection scheme would have to be cooked up—such as putting some of them in aircraft, or protecting the silos by an anti-ballistic missile (ABM) screen. Any system or combination of them would probably end up costing more than the original Carter scheme, but not in what Mr Reagan regards as the key 1983–84 budget years.

The political price could also be high. A new ABM system would mean altering the ABM treaty signed with Russia as part of Salt-1, which is one of the few solid achievements of arms controllers since 1945. It may not have been a very sensible achievement, since the ABMs could be a stabilising force in superpower nuclear competition, but any attempt to circumvent the treaty would be castigated as a new escalation of the arms race. Still, America should continue, at least, with more ABM research.

Mr Weinberger is sensibly keen to proceed at once with the MX. He also wants the B-1 bomber, which is not so sensible. He regards the B-1 as a stopgap manned bomber to replace the ageing B52s, for some of its more hazardous missions, until the Stealth (or advanced technology bomber, the ATB) is ready for production. The ATB is being designed to be almost undetectable by radar. Its development is going rather well, and it is now scheduled to be in service only three years after the B-1. Some $2.8 billion has been allocated towards both aircraft in the 1982 budget, though 100 B-1s would eventually cost over $20 billion.

Mr Weinberger should allow the B-1 to stay cancelled and try to speed production of the ATB. This would bring a net saving in the defence budget, including during the critical three years ahead when a B-1 targeted for 1986 service would be costly. The snag is that the B-1 has a powerful constituency. Almost every state in the union has a stake in its development. The air force would even support a delay in the ATB in order to save the B-1, hoping it would end up some day with both. The Reagan administration should shoot these lobbyists down.

One weapon which would cost little this side of the 1984 budget is the Trident-2 missile. This is a more accurate, longer-range replacement for the Trident-1, which is now in service as part of America's nuclear submarine deterrent. At present Russian anti-submarine techniques are nowhere near good enough to detect Trident submarines anywhere, so Trident-2's longer range is not needed. But Trident-2's development could be kept ticking over at fairly low cost, ready to rush into service if Russian detection methods display any breakthrough.

The Conventional Wish-Lists

Strategic forces account for only about 10% of America's military budget. General-purpose conventional forces take around 40%. By far the biggest expense in them is people. More money has already made a difference here: the quality of manpower in the armed services at last shows unmistakable signs of improving. Last year's pay rise (another is due in October) and higher morale have boosted recruiting and the rate at which experienced servicemen re-enlist. Pay will have to keep pace with inflation (at least) if this trend is to continue; as long as military pay does not exceed the gnp deflator, then wages (which account for 50% of defence spending) will not push up real defence costs.

Much of the extra cash for conventional forces in fiscal 1982 will be spent on the European central front, building up badly depleted stocks of spare parts and ammunition, etc. But Mr Reagan's defence aides are less Eurocentric than Mr Carter's. After improving America's nuclear capability, their next priority is the defence of the Middle East oilfields. In that the navy has a key role.

Mr John Lehman, the dynamic young secretary of the

navy, made a fast start. He won a commitment from the administration to a force of 15 aircraft carrier battle groups (an increase of three) and to a 600-ship navy before the other two services had loaded guns for their own offensives. The first new carrier will be included in the 1983 budget request along with some funding for the second.

The army, which wants a new division, and the air force, which wants at least one new air wing (around 72 aircraft), are now having to argue for them at a time when the talk is of cuts in planned spending. Has Mr Lehman been allowed to sail ahead too fast?

A 15-carrier fleet has been justified by the need to keep a task force in the Indian Ocean. It would be possible to manage with less. And a potent Rapid Deployment Force (RDF) might be a better deterrent to aggressors in that part of the world (which includes the Gulf) than the fact that the American navy has, somewhere in the world, 15 instead of 12 carrier battle groups. The naval build-up means heavy spending between now and 1984 and even heavier outlays after that. A bit of this should be sacrificed in order to pump money into the RDF, including bases near the Gulf.

The building of a 12-ship group of new pre-positioning ships to hold supplies in the Indian Ocean base at Diego Garcia is going ahead. More are needed, as well as extra troops— ideally marines—to ensure that an adequate RDF could be mustered and deployed without knocking a hole in the reserves available to Nato's central front. Above all, the RDF needs more long-range military transport—which should mean building more C-5As (the air force's present heavy-lift transport aircraft), rather than a new and expensive aircraft not ready for years.

After the RDF, the "wish-lists" of the three services add up to more than the kitty. So some careful choices must be made, especially over tactical aircraft. In recent years the procurement rates of these have slumped, thereby driving up unit costs, while failing to meet essential replacement needs. But aircraft are expensive beasts, and raising production rates to more efficient levels would cost billions in the short run till 1984.

One suggestion has been to cancel the navy's F-18/A-18 fighter-bomber, which has been dogged by development problems and a 20% increase in real costs. It is only now coming into production. Mr Carter's Pentagon would have been wise to order more F-14 fighters and A-6 and A-7 attack aircraft in their place, but the F-18 programme is now probably too far advanced. The best course for the long run would be to push up the procurement rates of all combat aircraft to economical levels—and to complete at least one production run as early as possible and then shut down that line. However, this would mean very heavy spending during the present five-year plan. If big cuts are made in the 1983–86 budgets the Pentagon will probably have to continue buying at uneconomical rates. The main priorities for higher spending should therefore be:

—Rapid development of the MX missile with protective arrangements of some kind. The B-1 to stay cancelled while research is speeded up on an ABM system for the MX and a new ATB and kept steady for Trident-2.

—Keeping forces' pay up to a level to get educated recruits.

—A beefed-up RDF.

—Restocking of depleted war reserves, and bringing repairs and maintenance up to date.

—Modest improvements in conventional weapons.

The main contributions to Mr Stockman's austerity drive should be to do without the B-1, to make a smaller naval build-up and to stop plumping for every new weapon that could be made available. That probably won't add up to a $30 billion cut in planned spending levels (outlays) between now and 1984, but Mr Stockman's full demand would cut the projected rate of increase ($90 billion) by a third and leave the Reagan administration spending only a fraction more than President Carter proposed. The full Stockman target could not be hit without making mockery of President Reagan's foreign policy rhetoric. Better to run a moderately unbalanced budget.

If Industry Cannot Cope . . .

Stagnant defence spending, while the real cost of weapons was rising sharply, has eroded industry's ability to cope with an upsurge in military buying now. The problem does not lie with major manufacturers. Many have enough excess capacity to cope with bigger defence budgets. But as defence work has dried up many subcontractors have drifted into other industries. In aerospace, the number of subcontractors fell from 6,000 in 1968 to 4,000 in 1976.

The results are: (a) huge delays in many vital parts (there is a 120-day delay in aluminum aircraft forgings, for example); (b) less competition, which pushes up costs to captive customers; (c) shortages of skilled workers beginning to develop. One estimate is that defence-related companies will have 10,000 unfilled vacancies for skilled workers by 1985. Firms will bid for skills, pushing up wage levels and eventually prices.

The big firms say that multi-year procurement by the Pentagon—guaranteeing a certain number of orders over a given period—would encourage companies to train more skilled labour and entice subcontractors back into defence work. Even without these privileges, a boost in defence spending will make life tough for some American engineering and electronic firms in the non-defence fields. They will be faced with rising costs and shortages in their industries.

This might matter less if America's allies were arming at the same rate as America, since allied industry would face the same bottlenecks. They are not doing so. The Americans are likely to grow increasingly tetchy about the loss of non-defence work to their allies because American industry is devoting more effort to defending the west.

America faces some painful cuts in other forms of government spending in its drive to rearm. The budget office has plans to raise the retirement age for all citizens to 68 and to base old-age pensions on a lower inflation index. This would help to make room for the extra defence spending, but there may also have to be second thoughts about some tax cuts made this year, such as the (too) generous investment allowances for business and the index-linking of income tax.

Talk, in consequence, of cutting costs in Europe's central front can already be heard among Republicans on Capitol Hill. Today's Republican party hails increasingly from the south and west, where isolationism has always been strong. It would be ironic if the price of a stronger America in the world was a weaker American commitment to western Europe. Such a prospect may be just the spur America's friends in Europe need to galvanise them against the growing neutralist tendencies which thwart their own defence efforts.

A DEFENSE BUDGET FOR THE 1980S[3]

The Pentagon has been aglow with anticipation since Ronald Reagan won the presidency. Broad smiles flash beneath every braided cap. The Army talks of tens of extra billions for new hardware in the next five years. The Navy dreams once again of three new carrier battle groups. At the Air Force, they're digging out plans for the long-dead B-1 bomber. The Marines think their latest hovercraft project might lift off, along with new missions and glory for the Corps. If wishes were weapons, in fact, the balance of power would thunder over to our side.

But it's not going to be that easy. Caspar Weinberger, Reagan's nominee as Secretary of Defense, is the same "Cap the Knife" who just weeks ago insisted that in order to fight inflation the whole federal budget must be sliced by $30 billion. Since that kind of money can't be wrung entirely out of "waste in government," Reagan's new Pentagon team won't

[3] Excerpt from a magazine article, "A Defense Budget for the 1980s," by Donald D. Holt, staff writer. FORTUNE magazine, 103:52–8. Ja. 26, '81. Copyright © 1981 Time Inc. All rights reserved. Reprinted by permission.

be able to do everything at once, even with the best of intentions spurred on by the greatest sense of urgency.

Reagan's defense transition team has been struggling with hard choices for weeks and is preparing to suggest that Reagan seek supplemental appropriations of at least $10 billion as an add-on to the budget for fiscal 1981, which began October 1. In this article, the last of three on U.S. defense needs, FORTUNE offers a defense proposal of its own, a rough-cut budget for the Eighties that corrects critical deficiencies, prepares for potential threats in a rational way, and stops short of becoming a runaway engine of inflation.

Our budget is hardly cheap. It calls for real growth at a rate of 7.3% a year through fiscal 1985, topping out at $219 billion in constant 1981 dollars. In that year, defense would be absorbing about 6.5% of GNP, vs. 5.5% today. Jimmy Carter, by comparison, had proposed raising spending by about 4.6% annually to $192 billion in 1985. Though Reagan never got specific, numbers leaking out of Reagan's camp before Election Day pointed toward annual growth of 9.2%, leading to a budget of around $239 billion by 1985.

In preparing the article, FORTUNE got valuable guidance from Lawrence J. Korb, director of defense-policy studies for the American Enterprise Institute, and William Kaufmann, a former Defense Department consultant who is a professor of political science at MIT and a consultant at the Brookings Institution. Neither is responsible for, nor necessarily agrees with, all of our conclusions.

The FORTUNE budget is divided into three broad categories: readiness, which lumps together funds for operations, maintenance, and the myriad consumables of war; major investment, for big-ticket items like aircraft carriers and intercontinental missile systems; and manpower, the biggest chunk.

The readiness category needs the quickest cash transfusion. By the Pentagon's own standards, much of the force is not ready to go to war. Six of the ten Army divisions in the U.S. lack the most mundane tools of war—truck parts, spare tires, rifle bullets. Nearly half the Air Force's fighter planes are not ready to fight.

This grim circumstance arose because of the way the Pentagon responded to the twin problems of a tightfisted Congress after Vietnam and soaring fuel prices. As the national mood of non-intervention grew, readiness seemed an obvious place to skimp. Why keep troops on tiptoe if they were unlikely to be sent into combat? The money saved could be used to develop major new weapons systems.

Perceptions changed with a bang after Iran and Afghanistan. The new awareness of danger was accompanied by the realization that the U.S. had little capacity to act. Certainly all crises can't be solved by sending in the troops (see "The Mental Gap in the Defense Debate," FORTUNE, September 8, 1980). On the other hand, without some kind of credible means to intervene in unstable situations, grand pronouncements like last winter's Carter Doctrine drawing the line in the Persian Gulf have a scary hollowness.

There's not much debate about what to buy. After years of neglect it's just a matter of filling up the bins with enough of what the services already use. But it's going to be expensive.

More training time is necessary too. Flying hours, steaming days, and maneuvering on the ground were all cut back. "We got pretty good at trimming operations to save money," says one general. "But we probably went too far." When pilots spend fewer hours in the air, morale drops, along with reenlistments, and the accident rate climbs.

Readiness spending will have to rise faster than the defense budget as a whole. FORTUNE calls for increases of about 10% a year, reaching $63.9 billion by 1985 (in 1981 dollars), compared with roughly $52 billion under Carter's projected program. Of that, $41.2 billion would go for operations and maintenance (not including paychecks for civilian mechanics, which we have put in the personnel category), and $22.7 billion for the bullets, torpedoes, and rockets in the item the Pentagon blandly calls "minor procurement."

The Case for the B-1

If it's hard to get into an argument these days over the need to increase readiness, it's hard to avoid one when it comes to major weapons. The amount of money involved is huge, and programs like the B-1 bomber or a new carrier battle group tend to shape defense strategy for years.

The first big defense Donnybrook of the Reagan Administration is likely to be over the B-1, killed by Carter four years ago. The Republican platform called for resuscitation of the program and there is every indication Reagan intends to try. Last time around, the debate turned into an emotional guns-vs.-butter morality play. There were candlelight vigils outside the Pentagon and demonstrators taunted executives of Rockwell International, the prime contractor, with placards denouncing them as "baby burners."

Now that the Vietnam hangover has just about worn off, it might be possible to consider the B-1 on its merits. Bombers take hours rather than minutes to cross continents, but unlike ICBMs they can be called back. Thanks to the wizardry of electronics, they can foil air defenses and strike targets in the Soviet heartland. As cruise-missile carriers, firing from outside the enemy's borders, they give us an additional form of mobile strategic response. They can be sent out to destroy a concentration of enemy ships far from shore—an important role if the U.S. is to keep the North Atlantic sea-lanes open in a major war. Bombers are also effective weapons in a small, conventional war.

All these tasks are currently assigned to the remarkably durable B-52, a subsonic plane built in the 1950s. But the B-52s are wearing out and will have to be replaced starting no later than 1990. So the question becomes which new bomber makes sense: the dormant B-1, or a start-from-scratch design including whatever advances in technology have occurred in the last four years, such as the radar-avoidance techniques dubbed "stealth."

The strongest argument for the B-1 is that it is nearly ready to go; the research and development was completed and several prototypes were built—all at a cost of $4.3 billion—before the project was shut down. If we could skip the B-1 and move on very quickly to a stealth bomber, that would be the smart course. But experience teaches that a new, sophisticated system always takes longer than expected, even on a crash basis. With the B-52s aging, this is just too big a risk to take. The best bet is to build a limited number of B-1s, incorporating some new technology, and push ahead on an all-new bomber to follow. Instead of an estimated $17 billion for enough planes to replace the B-52 fleet, we could buy 50 for $6 billion over the next five years. Then if stealth bogged down, we would have the option of building more B-1s.

The advanced version of the B-1, coming on line by 1986, would help deal with our most pressing strategic problem: the vulnerability of America's 1,000 Minuteman missiles. The Russians have improved the accuracy of their big missiles and by 1982 could theoretically destroy 80% of our ICBMs in a first strike.

Assuming that the Russians launched such a devastating first strike, our bombers would be the only surviving weapons with the accuracy needed to destroy the rest of the Soviet missiles in their hardened silos. To back up the fleet of 50 B-1s, FORTUNE proposes that the B-52 alert rate be increased from 30% to 40%, which would ensure that some 160 rather than 120 of the planes would be able to get off the ground before the Soviet missiles arrived. Increasing the alert rate would cost an estimated $200 million a year and give the Air Force some manpower problems. But that's a small price for sleeping more soundly. A simultaneous assault by the high-level B-52s and the supersonic, ground-skimming B-1s would vastly complicate Russia's air-defense problems, and the twin threat could divert scarce Soviet technological resources from more aggressive pursuits.

Closing the Window

Other, thoroughgoing solutions to that so-called "window" of vulnerability—meaning the years during which the

Russians theoretically could wipe out our ICBMs with a first strike—will be distressingly slow. After years of stalling, Carter called for deployment of the heavier, more accurate MX missile in a mobile basing arrangement that would protect it from the Russians. The missiles would lie on huge trucks and be moved around to various launching sites in Utah and Nevada. The Air Force put the cost at about $37 billion but it could shoot as high as $50 billion or more.

The MX is really two programs: the missile itself, which will give us more ability to kill Soviet missiles and other hard military targets, and the mobile-basing system designed to protect the MX against a first strike. The missile is worth all the dollars it will cost. But we ought to keep an open mind on the base arrangement.

The first problem is the complexity of the trucking system. "I am suspicious of lots of moving parts," says one expert. The sheer magnitude of the construction program—it would rival the interstate highway system—almost guarantees cost overruns. Even if the program is needed for the national defense, environmental groups could upset the schedule unless Congress was willing to override their lawsuits with the kind of sweeping legislation that finally got the Alaska pipeline going.

Defense analysts like Lawrence Korb are coming to think that we ought to stick with our old silos and protect them with an antiballistic-missile defense system, which used to be known as the ABM but now is called BMD. Such an approach has been largely ruled out since the U.S. and the Soviet Union signed a treaty limiting antiballistic-missile systems in 1972. But the time may be right to reopen the matter. As we improve our ability to hit their hard targets, the Russians may decide that instead of matching our mobile deployment to protect themselves, some kind of BMD system might be an easier and perhaps cheaper solution. The treaty comes up for its regular five-year review in 1982, which would be an opportune time to explore this question. If the Russians are obdurate, we have the option of abrogating the treaty on six months' notice—though that is obviously not a step to be taken lightly.

The technology has vastly improved since the treaty was signed. BMD experts now envision a two-tier system: in the upper atmosphere, missiles could be intercepted by rockets armed with conventional warheads. The missiles that got through would be attacked by a low-altitude defense network using minicomputers and nuclear-tipped interceptors at each missile site. On both these tiers, a near miss is as good as a kill, since it would jar the missiles from their newly devilish accuracy. FORTUNE allocates $200 million a year for stepped-up BMD research. As the more potent MX comes off the line, it could be stuffed into Minuteman silos. But even on optimistic assumptions, BMD wouldn't close the "window" before 1990.

Van Cleave's Shell Game

Various schemes have been proposed to close the window more quickly. William Van Cleave, head of Reagan's defense transition team, wants to dig additional holes near existing Minuteman silos. The Minutemen in our arsenal would then be moved among the holes in what has come to be called the "shell game." When the MX is ready, we could dig more holes and play a shell game with them too.

The shell game complicates arms-control negotiations— which FORTUNE assumes will go forward under Reagan—because neither side would be able to verify how many missiles were in all those holes. But some critics think the Russians could find out, through spies or other means. If they did, the missiles would be vulnerable because moving them to other silos would be slow and clumsy.

Other defense experts have turned against the shell game quick fix on the mundane grounds that it wouldn't be quick at all. They argue that in a contentious, environmentally conscious country, the MX will be coming off the line before the land could be acquired and the silos built to accommodate Van Cleave's shell game.

Since sheep ranchers or wheat farmers might be able to hold up either the shell game or a mobile MX, we ought to hedge the bet. The sea-based leg of the nuclear triad is the least accurate but also the least vulnerable member. The sub-based missiles can't destroy Soviet silos, but in an all-out nuclear exchange, they might be all that we have left for the second stage of a war for survival.

The Trident submarine, the replacement for the Polaris subs now nearing the end of their useful lives, is supposed to come off the line at the rate of one a year. General Dynamics is having trouble meeting that target (the first sub, due next spring, may be months late). The funding ought to be stepped up to three subs every two years to reach a total of 25 by the early 1990s. Since the Tridents carry more warheads, they would give us more punch.

In addition, the development of the Trident II missile ought to be accelerated to permit deployment by the end of the decade. This heavier, more accurate missile would nearly match the hard-target capability of the MX. The cost of accelerating both programs would be $4.8 billion above what Carter projected.

Winnebagos for the Army

In conventional investment, the Army has so much ground to make up that it has begun throwing around the kind of boxcar numbers normally associated with big strategic or shipbuilding programs. "Congress loves to build airplanes," says one budget analyst. "But it never wants to build anything for the Army." There's just no romance in the gritty equipment the Army uses. A contract for tank treads doesn't stir a Congressman's soul.

The Army has a long shopping list known as the Big Seven: the XM-1 battle tank, an armored troop carrier called the infantry fighting vehicle (IFV), two new helicopters, and three new air-defense systems. Some critics say the list grew so long because the Army has been glacial in figuring out how its new weapons ought to perform. The IFV has been on the drawing board nearly ten years and the result is a cumbersome vehicle described by one wit as an "off-the-road Winnebago." The gas-turbine engine of the XM-1 tank is still causing problems, and full-scale production is just about to begin, nearly two years behind schedule.

The time has come to get moving. The Army has at least a dozen answers for each dozen criticisms. Even if some flaws remain in these major weapons, they have already been studied half to death. The designs ought to be frozen so the hardware can be kicked out the door in huge quantities. Carter budgeted $15 billion for Army investment over five years. FORTUNE would double that.

One item that isn't in our budget for the Army is equipment to be used in the Rapid Deployment Force. The RDF was created by Carter last winter in response to rising tensions in the Persian Gulf. In an emergency the RDF, now consisting only of a headquarters unit, would be fleshed out with previously designated Army and Marine units—up to 200,000 men—and moved quickly into a trouble spot. The need for rapid deployment is real enough, but the idea of mixing Marine and Army units under one command worries a lot of people, especially in Congress. It has never worked well before, and it probably won't work in the RDF.

The mission ought to be turned over to the Marines, which have been the nation's RDF for 200 years. That would make better use of the Corps, a unique entity in the world of arms. At 188,000 men, it is bigger than the British Army.

Army critics argue that the Marines are too lightly armed to do much more than seize and hold a beach until the Army arrives. "If you want to make the Marines just like the Army," says one senior Army commander with heavy sarcasm, "it can become the RDF." The Marines counter that their lack of heavy armor and artillery is easily made up for by tactical air. A new light tank would give the Marines more punch on the ground. The Army would not be out of the picture. Any sustained conflict would require massive reinforcements. But the Marine and Army units would arrive sequentially, keeping command lines straight.

The Navy Craves Carriers

As world tensions rise, the Navy's aircraft carriers are bearing the brunt of the U.S. craving for military presence. The Navy is naturally pushing to get to 16 carrier battle groups, up by three.

More carriers would obviously make the Navy's job easier. But each battle group requires some 18 companion ships, and with a full load of planes on the carrier, that comes to around a $10-billion investment for each group. Nobody knows how long the carriers would last in an all-out conventional war if Soviet Backfire bombers were able to find them. Thus their main purpose is demonstrating U.S. power in tense situations. The cost is unacceptable given all the other needs, including the Navy's desires for many other kinds of ships and aircraft.

FORTUNE's shipbuilding program would be bigger than Carter's proposals for the next five years. At an added cost of nearly $3 billion a year, we would build enough ships to hold the basic fleet at its present size while adding a lot of punch in special categories. The FORTUNE budget would buy eight more big Los Angeles-class attack subs to keep sea-lanes open, more amphibious vessels, and more fast cargo ships. The last two categories would give more sea-lift to the Marines.

We would also add significantly to Navy air, which Chief of Naval Operations Thomas Hayward says is his biggest deficiency. The Navy needs 300 planes a year just to stay even, but it has been getting only a bit more than half that many. The cost of keeping even is an additional $1.6 billion a year.

The Air Force too is short of fighters. The problem for both services is simplified by the fact that the production lines are running. Output should be stepped up significantly; when that is done, unit costs come down. To fill out its authorized 26 air wings, the Air Force should spend $1 billion more annually over the next five years, building 240 more F-16s and 60 more A-10s.

A stickier question is what kind of new transport, if any,

should be put in production for rapidly deploying troops. The Air Force is pushing for a dream plan dubbed the CX, which would be a wide-body capable of landing on, say, a flat golf course, or in a desert. The Air Force asked for $6 billion to buy the plane but has yet to back up the request with a believable design.

Given all the other things the Air Force needs, the best idea is to make the most of existing aircraft. The Air Force should complete its plans to stretch its existing C-141s (which will yield carrying power equivalent to 90 more planes), buy 20 more of Lockheed's huge and speedy C-5s, and push ahead with modifications of the existing C-5s to add years to their service lives.

To get more lift in an emergency, the Air Force should expand a program called CRAF (Civil Reserve Air Fleet), in which 747s and DC-10s operated by the airlines are strengthened so that in a pinch they could carry heavy military equipment. At $10 million each, the overhauls are a bargain, but the Air Force has so far put up funds for converting only 14 planes. We would increase that to 50 over the next five years. The government has to pay an operating subsidy, because the added weight increases fuel consumption. But the Pentagon pays nothing for maintenance or crews, so the planes amount to a large, cheap airlift reserve.

College for the Troops

Big systems like the MX missile command attention, but the largest, most intractable chunk of the defense budget is the mundane business of paying the troops in an all-volunteer force.

When the volunteer army pegged a private's pay 11% above the minimum wage, plus the usual benefits, soldiering became just another job, an alternative to the assembly line or the checkout counter. Quotas were filled in those first years, but as inflation swelled civilian paychecks, the services fell far behind. Now the all-volunteer force is clearly in trouble.

After falling short in 1979, the services eked out their quotas last year with the help of a recession. The Army had to lower its standards, taking more recruits in the lowest mental category.

One obvious answer would be a return to the draft. Supporters of the draft like Senator Sam Nunn argue that it is more equitable and would supply the mix of aptitudes the services need. If we had to increase the force level dramatically, a draft would seem imperative, but for now, with Reagan opposed, it is simply not in the cards. One thing that should be done to make the volunteer force work is a revision of the pay scales. Scarce missile technicians should earn more than cooks and drivers of the same rank.

To spur recruitment, we should bring back the GI Bill. Manpower specialists at the Pentagon dismiss the GI Bill as "a form of nostalgia" and build their plans around higher enlistment bonuses. But while money is important, college benefits would attract ambitious, upwardbound recruits, the sort the Army needs. To work, this new GI Bill has to be good. FORTUNE proposes a program that would pay up to $14,800 if a student attended four years at a state university, and up to $22,800 if he or she went to a private college. Since nobody knows how many veterans would use such benefits, the expense is hard to calculate. FORTUNE estimates the cost at around $2 billion a year.

If the country is serious about encouraging national service without compulsion, it could make up some of the costs by reducing existing federal loan and scholarship programs that pay for college tuition. As with all such programs, most of the subsidies go to middle-class kids. They could get even more generous benefits if they wanted to earn them by enlisting for three years.

It's Affordable

This defense budget is hardly perfect, but it gives us a chance to rebuild our forces without also heating the economy into hyper-inflation. If the program sounds expensive, and it is, consider a few large round numbers. The Carter plan, which now looks inadequate, would have allocated $885 billion to defense over the five-year period. The FORTUNE program costs $85 billion more than that but $145 billion less than the program Reagan seems to be endorsing. If Reagan achieves his minimum goals in curbing nondefense spending (an outcome described as "partial achievement" in his preliminary economic program), the FORTUNE proposal would provide room for $324 billion in tax cuts over the five-year period, compared with $158 billion in tax cuts under the Democratic program which allows more for nondefense programs.

Reagan will soon have to make hard choices between the tax-cutting and defense-spending wings of his Administration. He will obviously have to compromise, though not necessarily along the lines of this FORTUNE proposal. If the Joint Chiefs are disappointed at not getting all their dreams fulfilled, they should take solace from one important fact. They'll be getting one more defense program they won't have to pay for, at least not with a line item. A strong economy has to be the first line of defense.

WE SPEND TOO MUCH ON DEFENSE[4]

Ronald Reagan has come to power on a platform of alleged United States military weakness and imminent world dominance by the Soviet Union. Mr. Reagan calls for huge increases in military spending as the chief means of showing the world that the nation is still No. 1. The military budget is again to be used as the central symbol of America's world role.

Any assessment of military budgets must acknowledge

[4] Excerpt from a newspaper article "We Spend Too Much on Defense," by Gene R. LaRocque, retired rear admiral and director of the Center for Defense Information. *The New York Times*, Sec. 3, p.3. F. 1, '81. Copyright © 1981 by The New York Times Company. Reprinted by permission.

that they are first of all political instruments in the hands of American leaders. No clear relationship has been established between the level of military spending and measurable calculations of national security, victory in battle or deterrence of conflict.

The vagaries of public opinion, political interests and media attention have more to do with budgets than strictly military considerations. The military budget is formed to accord with the mood of the American electorate, and is shaped by the American political process. There is little that is indisputedly rational or inevitable about it, but there is much that a consensus of habit and custom has sanctified. From year to year, the latest fad of military strategy or foreign policy prevents tinkering at the edges.

Today, the military budget is more than ever the victim of changing circumstances. The budget is increasingly utilized as a vehicle for sending "messages" and "symbols" of will and intention. However, because we do not understand the rest of the world very well and the rest of the world certainly does not understand us very well, the military budget as a symbol is even less effective than the military budget as a measure of our real defense capability.

Too many extensive programs are competing in the military arena and even the budget increases contemplated by the Reagan Administration cannot accommodate all of them. We cannot simultaneously acquire a vast new arsenal of nuclear weapons, expand costly forces for defending countries in Europe and Asia, add to substantial equipment and manpower for rapid intervention everywhere in the world, enlarge a very expensive Navy for deployment on all the world's oceans, develop new weapons that are always better than Soviet weapons and keep existing forces at a high level of readiness and training.

The most unneeded feature of the new budget is its stepped-up pursuit of nuclear weaponry. Mr. Reagan and his advisers have stated that their first priority is a "quick fix" of nuclear forces. Their plans include an expanded MX missile program, revival of a manned bomber, additions to the existing Minuteman missile force, acceleration of the Trident II submarine-based missile, speeded deployment of new Trident submarines, increased spending on antiballistic-missile programs, and accelerated and expanded new nuclear-tipped Cruise and Pershing missiles for deployment in Europe. Mr. Reagan's new Deputy Secretary of Defense, Frank Carlucci, has summed up this nuclear expansion program in claiming that the United States must develop a "nuclear war-fighting capability." As Mr. Carlucci admits, "that's a very large order."

But programs like the proposed MX missile and new nuclear missiles for Europe do not enhance our security. They contribute little to the defense of the United States and are probably harmful. New nuclear missiles do not help to secure oil supplies or promote the resolution of international turbulence. They are irrelevant to most real-world problems.

Obsession with extremely remote scenarios for fighting nuclear war at a time when the nation has other clear and present dangers distracts us from taking those realistic steps that are genuinely needed for national defense.

"Quick fixes" in the area of nuclear weaponry will waste tens of billions of dollars over the next decade. These billions will likely come at the expense of other programs, both military and nonmilitary, which could contribute far more to the defense and well-being of America.

The first priority for military expenditures should be insuring that the existing military establishment, including personnel and weapons, is utilized in the most appropriate and efficient manner. Of course, this only sounds like common sense and everyone rhetorically endorses the proposition. However, we cannot underestimate the power of the ingrained habit of undervaluing what we already have in pursuit of fancy new weapons incorporating the newest features of technology. The rush to produce these new aircraft, ships, tanks and missiles will inevitably lead to neglect of weapons already in the field. Congress and the American people, even in the current pro-defense climate, can only be brought to provide the funds for very expensive new weapons if they are convinced of the alleged inadequacies of existing weapons. . . .

The economic costs of military power are great. The real present danger is rampant inflation that affects every American, and there should be strong pressures to contain all aspects of government spending. We must strive to maintain some sense of balance about our military and foreign policy problems. As Thomas Ross, who was Mr. Carter's Assistant Secretary of Defense for Public Affairs, recently said, "The military is getting such a favorable hearing that there is a danger that everything that drops from their lips will be taken as holy writ." The 1980 election-year rhetoric about American weakness could lead to an extremely wasteful period of throwing money at military problems. Overstatements of problems usually lead to overreactions and most frequently to "solutions" that offer no real solution.

The United States has strong and wealthy allies who today can more than ever look after their own defense. Consultation with our military allies to achieve a redistribution of the burdens of defense must be undertaken. This is a necessary component of a Western campaign to slow inflation in the world economy.

The sensible areas of military investment in the coming years are increased military pay, more funding for military readiness and maintenance of existing weapons, more spending on noncarrier Naval forces (particularly for antisubmarine warfare), greater procurement of proven existing weapons (such as A-10 antitank aircraft and antitank missiles), enhanced protection for sea-based strategic nuclear forces and adequate funding for fundamental and advanced military research and development. If we are to do what is required in these areas, we will have to be tough-minded in rejecting many other proposed military programs.

It is difficult to measure how much military spending is enough. But it is clear that spending is excessive if the nation's political, social or economic fabric is weakened in the process.

A CRITICAL VIEW OF THE U.S.
MILITARY ESTABLISHMENT[5]

Playing "What's wrong with the military?" has become a favorite American game since the embarrassing failure of the Tehran rescue mission. Some of the least encouraging answers come from Edward N. Luttwak, a professional military analyst who has been a consultant to the Secretary of Defense and is the author of nine books and studies of war. The senior fellow at the Georgetown Center for Strategic & International Studies has criticized the raid to free the hostages in Tehran, not because of the effort but because of its apparent ineptness. FORBES put some simple questions to Luttwak and got some pessimistic answers.

Luttwak: Let's start with the things that are hard and physical. The fighter planes of the Air Force, are they ready to fly? Are the ships ready to sail? Are the radar and the missile launchers ready to function? Are they maintained? We all know it's very expensive in manpower and spare parts to keep everything working 100%, 100% of the time. Readiness is very perishable; like French bread, you have to buy it every day, it doesn't last. So 100% readiness would be terribly wasteful, but we have to keep the whole machine going at considerably better than zero. The question is, how much? For this purpose targets are laid down.

Let's say 70% to 80% of top fighters in Europe are to be ready at all times. Maybe in the States it is 60%, ready to fly. When you look at what they want, you find a big gap. In practice if the U.S. has 400 F-15 fighters, to make up a number, it has only 150 ready to fly. This means you are spending a lot of money to buy aircraft you don't actually have. They are on the lists but not actually available to shoot. This is a straightforward problem, the consequence of lack of money.

[5] Reprinted from a magazine article, "A critical view of the U.S. military establishment," by Edward N. Luttwak, Senior Fellow at the Georgetown Center for Strategic & International Studies. *Forbes*, 125:37–9. My. 26, '80. Reprinted by permission of FORBES Magazine from the May 26, 1980 issue. Copyright © 1980 Forbes Inc.

In the Air Force, it may be lack of money for spare parts and technicians. In the Navy it is a huge shortage of technicians. The Navy is supposedly short 10,000 to 15,000 technically trained petty officers and men. Naval aviation is hit both ways, short of people and spare parts. But we are talking here only of the physical readiness of equipment.

There is a second question. Are these people combat-ready in the sense that they have the training, the experience, the discipline to actually fight? Here the picture varies considerably from service to service. The low average mental level of Army enlisted manpower and the practice of the Army to send its better people into maintenance and support and management and administration, leaving only the dregs for the combat units, means that what we have in those units are very simple people using very complicated equipment. The only way you can do this is with very, very rigorous training. But they don't do very much training. They mainly sit around in barracks because training is expensive. If it's artillery you have to shoot it. If it's armor you have to move it and shoot. So you have people of low mental categories who don't do much training spending a lot of time sitting around the barracks and therefore don't have the competence. They don't have the morale and the discipline, which is a function of morale. People who are bored and idle will not be disciplined.

The Army, therefore, is in very bad shape. It seems the Marine Corps is getting better manpower, more dedicated, more motivated, and spending more of its money on more intensive and more interesting training.

In the case of the Navy, it's a mixed picture. Apparently the Navy is badly afflicted by the loss of highly trained technical men and the cascade effect—if you're short of technicians, those left have to work harder, spend more time at sea, and this creates more unhappiness, which leads to more shortage.

The Air Force has much less of this problem. They are just short of money for spare parts, and in the case of the Strategic Air Command, short of money for fuel to fly their planes.

FORBES: But isn't this just the problem of the peacetime military? *Any* peacetime military?

Luttwak: That is almost an excuse. The truth is, we are in the position of someone who is trying to drive a car, a very powerful car, trying to drive it sideways. You can't do it. Sure, we are spending $150 billion, but we are spending in a way that is structurally wrong. You see, there are only a certain number of ways you can get men and train them into units.

One way is if you have national conscription. As a matter of course every 18-year-old knows and expects that when he reaches his birthday he will go into the service.

Another way is to have a truly professional army where you set very high standards for admission and you pay very well. That way you pick and choose and wind up with wonderful manpower and have no training or discipline problems. This is what the Indians do. It is a very poor country, and although the pay of soldiers is low by our standards, by India's standards it is high. So they have a truly professional army and get the very best of the population volunteering.

The third kind is to pick up the dregs of society, scouring the saloons, dragging them off the streets and out of the prisons. But then you have iron discipline, court martials, no appeals, corporal punishment. You make up with iron discipline what you don't have from motivation or enthusiasm.

The current American military force does not have mass conscription, does not have the high standards and selectivity of a truly professional army and does not have the discipline of an 18th-century army. It falls between alternatives and is not workable. You can only try to get capability to drowning the problem in money, but we're not drowning it in money. If we wanted to have a really effective army, with the present structure of the volunteer army we'd have to spend $250 billion a year, not $150 billion. The volunteer army is the most expensive way of getting true combat capability. It doesn't work.

FORBES: Doesn't our technological advantage, better weaponry, make up for those problems?

Luttwak: Technology or no technology, in the reality of warfare as opposed to paper calculations, the intangibles of leadership, command experience, tactical ingenuity, morale and skill of troops are much more important than materiel factors, your firepower, mobility and so on. It's not that these intangibles—from leadership to skill—will make the difference of 10% around the margin. From everything we know about warfare, ancient and modern, these intangibles easily dominate. It's not 10% around the margin, it's more like 200% to 300%.

You have to realize this is a very gadget-oriented society and the military share in this fascination. We have so many physicists and engineers prominent in our top defense policymaking and they, of course, wildly overestimate the important of gadgets. Every time we finally come to confront the reality of the Soviet armored threat, we think seriously for a while until somebody comes up with a new gadget that will solve the problem.

A few years ago there was much talk of these wire-guided [antitank] missiles. We'll get a few thousand of them with a few thousand men and they'll go behind a few thousand trees and we'll pick off the Russians as they come. Unfortunately, in war the technical is dominated by the tactical. The perfect wire-guided-missile kill rate of 90% goes to 50%, 40%, 30% or 20% when the other fellow is shooting at the fellow with the missile. And the armor is working to come behind you, and then the missile suddenly operates at 10%.

That we have all these engineers and physicists in our defense policymaking, men who are so enamored of technical solutions, is a disservice because it distracts from the real problem. A broadly capable armed enemy, like the Soviet army, with its tanks, with its artillery, with its mechanized infantry, with its gas forces, will not be defeated by devices of narrow ingenuity, by gimmicks like the wired missile or the assault breaker. The assault breaker is the latest gadget. You just instrument the battlefield and you sit behind and press buttons and all these missiles will come down and kill everything moving on it.

FORBES: Yet our equipment used in combat by allies such as the Israelis has been superior on the battlefield.

Luttwak: You mention the Israelis. If you look at the American defense establishment, it is full of engineers and some systems analysts. The Israeli defense establishment consists largely of soldiers on one hand and clerks on the other. The clerks, who are engineers and scientists, serve as advisers, strictly subordinate, at lower levels. It's not incorrect to say that American equipment has been operated better by the Israelis than by the U.S., and deployed better, too.

The problem is, and I am talking as a civilian analyst, that there is a deformity, a real deformity at the very center of our defense establishment. Serious study of warfare, on the art of warfare, has been suppressed by the brutal imposition of analytical techniques which measure wonderfully what they measure but which don't happen to measure the really significant aspects of war.

The tactical, the leadership, the morale, the skill, are so much more important than the material things. Yet the different techniques we use, the systems analysis, the programming, all capture only the material aspects.

FORBES: For example?

Luttwak: An example: Every person who has seriously studied war knows that it is critically important to allow the combat unit to develop kinship and solidarity. Men under fire don't fight for their country, they fight for their buddies. Everyone knows this and every serious army makes it a point to have very stable structures, regiments and the like. But that is not efficient. For simple efficiency you want to have all the manpower in a big pool and send the correctly trained person where he is needed most. But when you move the guy, you are disrupting two organizations; and there is no way you can put the morale—the terribly important but completely unmeasurable development of solidarity—into those computers.

If you look at our Army units, you'll see what enormous turbulence there is. People come and go all the time. Companies, battalions, platoons are not the homes of men, not a social group at all; they are just an administrative box into which manpower is flown in and out. This is one of many different examples of the same phenomenon, efficiency versus effectiveness. The conflict between civilian efficiency and military effectiveness runs right down the organization. Conflict is different from civilian activity, and leadership in war is totally different from management. Our people are managers in uniform. Actually, the American armed forces are very efficient; they just aren't very effective.

FORBES: Would you have any evidence for that?

Luttwak: The whole Vietnam War. During the entire conflict the efficiency of American military organizations was constantly manifested. The efficiency of communications, the efficiency with which firepower was administered, the efficiency of transportation and distribution, of medical services; but it was just not an effective war machine. The firepower, so efficiently administered, was not effective because the enemy refused to assemble in conveniently targetable massed formations. Less-efficient and less-managerial officers would have worked to find a method of war capable of dealing with people who refuse to assemble in conveniently targetable massed formations instead of concentrating on improving the efficiency of their firepower.

Armies are not efficient; armies are horribly inefficient; armies are wasteful, and so it should be.

FORBES: What should we do?

Luttwak: Shake them up a little. Come to grips with the fact that this country hasn't carried out a single major successful military operation in the last 30 years. [He mentions the Inchon landing in the Korean War as being that last success.] Accept this fact instead of pushing it under the rug.

The second part is to realize that the armed forces have deviated from the true study, exercise and tactics of warfare and become managerial institutions, largely concerned with the management of personnel and equipment, contemptuous of the art of war and indifferent to everything that is of war, like tactics and operations. Recognize these things and then move on reform.

FORBES: Such as?

Luttwak: One, for example, would be to reduce the number of officers. [He notes there is one officer today for each 6.4 enlisted men, including noncoms.] Or better still, greatly increase the manpower but don't increase the officers. These officers are layer upon layer upon layer of management, which slows initiative, slows decisionmaking, complicates any development. Now we have a queue of ten people wanting to command each battalion. The way we accommodate them is that the tours of commanders are very short. This prevents the unit from stabilizing under a leader. It violates good military practice.

FORBES: Why do you criticize the raid on Iran?

Luttwak: It was an unsound military plan that contradicts the four magic rules for commando operations.

One: Take a man's force to do a boy's job. Because you are inferior overall, you must be very superior at the point of contact; 97 Germans against 4 terrorists at Mogadishu [the commando attack on a hijacked airliner in Somalia]; 150 Israeli troops against 60 Ugandans.

Two: Combat risks being so high, no technical risk whatsoever is acceptable. If you land in fragile helicopters and you need 6, you take 12, 18—not 8.

Three. In all commando operations there is only one commander and he is on the spot. He doesn't need satellite communications because the only information he can send back is so sketchy and vague that any direction he gets from above is bound to mislead.

Four: The abandonment of the dead, of secret documents and intact helicopters is contrary to all the customs of war and the usages of the service. This has a powerful effect in intensifying the great loss of prestige that the country has suffered as a result of this debacle. A powerful effect. God knows how many Israeli commando operations have failed over the years, aborted. God knows, but the enemies of the Israelis don't, because the Israelis left no tracks.

This plan was a manifestation of the perverted use of military power, a perversion of the rules, the stripping of the combat content from a commando operation, which must be a combat operation by nature.

THE CASE FOR MILITARY REFORM[6]

Both major candidates in the presidential campaign put heavy stress on the need for a stronger defense. President Reagan is committed to increasing the defense budget, possibly by as much as $25 billion to $35 billion annually. But will increased spending really strengthen America's defenses?

The answer is: not necessarily. If the Reagan administration is serious about efforts to strengthen the military, it will have to look beyond the size of the budget. It will have to embrace a cause that has quietly been growing among defense academics and writers, officers in the field and a few elected officials: the cause of military reform.

Military reform means three basic changes:

It means spending more, selectively, for defense.

It means allocating funds to innovative weapons and programs.

And it means addressing a number of non-budgetary problems which, although not related to defense spending, relate directly to winning or losing wars. This includes re-examination of basic defense doctrine and concepts.

Underfunded Defense

First, we do need to increase the defense budget. Major elements in our defense establishment have been underfunded for some time. These include shipbuilding, military pay, operations and maintenance and strategic forces.

Second, we must direct our spending toward innovative

[6] Reprinted from a newspaper article "The Case for Military Reform," by Gary Hart, U.S. Senator (D-Colorado). *Wall Street Journal*, p.20. Ja. 23, '81. Reprinted by permission of the *Wall Street Journal*. Copyright © Dow Jones & Company, Inc., 1981. All Rights Reserved.

weapons and programs. Just spending more will not solve our problems. We risk being like the French in the 1930s, debating how much to spend each year on the Maginot Line.

If *what* we are buying will not work on the battlefield, then it does not matter how much of it we have.

Perhaps the Navy provides the best example of the need to spend our money for innovation. In the era when new weapons have made every surface ship significantly more vulnerable than it was 20 or even 10 years ago, the Navy has become dependent on just 13 ships—the 13 large aircraft carriers. Most other types of surface ships—cruisers and destroyers—are not only wedded to the aircraft carrier, they are themselves more vulnerable and increasingly less able to carry out their escort mission.

New concepts and technologies could free the Navy from many of its current problems. Vertical/short take-off and landing (V/STOL) aircraft could permit us to build smaller, less expensive carriers in much larger numbers. Modern diesel-electric submarines could complement our extremely expensive nuclear attack subs, enabling us to afford a much larger submarine force. Hydrofoils and surface effect ships could provide the high speeds—up to 80 knots—needed for truly effective anti-submarine ships. But this means spending our naval dollars in innovative ways, which we haven't been doing.

The third basic component of military reform, the need to attack some non-budgetary defense problems, is seldom addressed in our national defense debate. But these problems may be the most serious of all.

Our concept of land warfare is a good example. The doctrine of the Army still reflects the post-World War I French concept of a war of attrition dominated by massive firepower. Its object is to destroy the enemy physically, tank by tank and man by man.

The Germans demonstrated in World War II that a concept based on maneuver is more effective, especially for the side with fewer men and less equipment. The Russians learned maneuver warfare the hard way, from the Germans in World War II. We still haven't learned it. One can place the U.S. Army's field manuals side-by-side with those of the French in 1940 and find remarkable parallels. Unless we re-examine our entire concept of land warfare, it won't do much good merely to spend more money to buy more hardware.

The military education and promotion system is another example of a serious non-budgetary weakness. The military education system—the service academies, the command and staff schools, the war colleges—gives little attention to *ideas* about warfare. It emphasizes the study of management and lower-level leadership, not military history.

Promotion reinforces the effects of poor education. The services value the manager, tolerate the troop leader, but have virtually no place for the theorist.

We must give our officers a chance to think about warfare, both in our service schools and while on regular duty assignments. This means changes in the schools' curricula, including much greater emphasis on military history and theory, and possibly lengthening the school terms. It means upgrading and revitalizing our military journals. It means reducing the administrative load on the officer in the field, to give him time to think. And we should consider providing a formal career path for those officers who excel in military theory, to parallel those already existing for the troop leader and the manager.

Why have there not been stronger efforts from within the armed forces to create a place for the military theorist? This brings up what is perhaps our most fundamental military weakness: The armed services have in large part become bureaucracies.

Traditionally, the forces were organized on a "corporative" model. Each officer was inculcated with, and worked in every way to advance, the overall goals and purposes of his service. Today, only the Marine Corps adheres to this model.

Narrow Outlook

The Army, Navy and Air Force have instead adopted the bureaucratic model, in which the officer specializes in one or several narrow functions, and the overall goals of the institutions are supposedly attained by linking the "boxes" which define each individual's job. Unfortunately the narrow outlook this produces often causes those overall goals to be forgotten, while decisions are based on what the institutions find comfortable—which is to say, what they have done in the past.

If we are to avoid the military dangers this trend toward bureaucratization could cause, we must reform the very basis of our armed services—the way they make decisions—while we also reform specific military concepts and force structures, military education and the promotion system. Otherwise, the other reforms will only be temporary, for the ongoing process of change and adaptation which must characterize an effective military will not develop. This may be the single most challenging defense task we face.

Military reform presents a difficult challenge to the new administration. But it also offers an enormous opportunity. It offers a new basis for something we lost in Vietnam—a genuine national consensus on defense. There is nothing ideological about the issue. It is a task in which liberals and conservatives can join. It will indeed require a joining of those who have differed in the past. But if we are willing to think new thoughts, and see today's problems in the light of present realities, not as reflections of debates long past, it can be done.

8

ited States Congress. U.S. security assistance and arms transfer policies for the 1980s. Staff report to the Committee on Foreign Affairs, 97th Congress; 1st session, 1981. Supt. of Docs. Washington, D.C. 20402. '81.

ted States Congress. Office of Technology Assessment. The effects of nuclear war. Allanheld, Osmun & Co. '80.

ed States Department of Defense. Report of Secretary of Defense Harold Brown to the Congress on the FY 1982 budget, FY 1983 authorization request, and FY 1982–1986 defense programs, Ja. 19, '81.

ed States Department of Defense. Soviet military power. Supt. of Docs. Washington, D.C. 20402. '81.

PERIODICALS

Foreign Policy and Defense Review. 2:2. Jl. '80. The FY 981–1985 defense program; issues and trends. L.J. Korb. The merican Enterprise Institute for Public Policy Research. 150 17th St. N.W. Washington, D.C. 20036.

oreign Policy and Defense Review. 2:2&3. O. '81. Forces of bit: budgeting for tomorrow's fleets. J.W. Abellera and Rolf ark.

ontrol Today. 11:4. Ap. '81. Reviving the ABM debate. Carnesale. The Arms Control Association. 11 Dupont Cir- N.W. Washington, D.C. 20036.

247:21–33. My. '81. America's high-tech weaponry. J.M. ows.

248:7–8+. Ag. '81. Defense, taxes, and the budget. J.M. ows.

Week and Space Technology. 114:85–7. Ja. 19, '81. Perry Pentagon accomplishments. P.J. Klass.

Week and Space Technology. 114:35. F. 9, '81. Navy details loss of U.S. edge on Soviets.

Week and Space Technology. 114:200–1+. Ap. 27, '81. nse Dept. lists top 100 contractors for fiscal 1980.

f the Atomic Scientists. 36:23–7. Je. '80. Dollars or : the CIA's military estimates. F.D. Holzman.

the Atomic Scientists. 36:41–3. Je. '80. Scientists and ns procurement. Kosta Tsipis.

the Atomic Scientists. 37:12–13. My. '81. Reagan's de- udget. J. Isaacs.

eek. p. 80–4+. F. 4, '80. Defense production gap: why . can't rearm fast.

BIBLIOGRAPHY

An asterisk (°) preceding a reference indicates that the article or part of it has been reprinted in this book.

BOOKS AND PAMPHLETS

Adams, Gordon and Quinn, Geoff. The iron triangle. Council on Economic Priorities. 84 Fifth Ave., New York, N.Y. 10011. '81.

American Friends Service Committee. Questions & answers on the Soviet threat and national security. Disarmament Program. American Friends Service Committee. 1501 Cherry Street. Philadelphia, Pa. 19102. '81.

Barlow, J. G., ed. Reforming the military. The Heritage Foundation. 513 C St. N.E. Washington, D.C. 20002. '81.

Barnet, R.J. Real security: restoring American power in a dangerous decade. Simon & Schuster. '81.

Barton, J. H. The politics of peace: an evaluation of arms control. Stanford University Press. '81.

Caldicott, Helen. Nuclear madness. Bantam. '80.

Carnegie Panel on U.S. Security and the Future of Arms Control. Challenges for U.S. national security; assessing the balance: defense spending and conventional forces. A preliminary report, part II. Carnegie Endowment for International Peace. '81.

Carnegie Panel on U.S. Security and the Future of Arms Control. Challenges for U.S. national security; defense spending and the economy; the strategic balance and strategic arms limitation. A preliminary report. Carnegie Endowment for International Peace. '81.

CBS News. CBS reports: the defense of the United States; June 14, 15, 16, 17, 18, 1981. CBS News. 524 West 57th St. New York, N.Y. 10019. '81.

Center for Defense Information. U.S. military force—1980; an evaluation. Center for Defense Information. 122 Maryland Ave. N.E. Washington, D.C. 20002.

Central Intelligence Agency. National Foreign Assessment Center. Soviet and U.S. defense activities. 1971–80: a dollar cost comparison. Central Intelligence Agency. Washington D.C. 10505. '81.

Chace, James. Solvency: the price of survival. Random. '81.

"Cincinnatus." Self-destruction: the disintegration of the United States army during the Vietnam era. Norton. '81.

Cline, R.S. World power trends and U.S. foreign policy for the 1980s. Westview Press. '80.

Coffey, Kenneth. Strategic implications of the all-volunteer force: the conventional defense of central Europe. University of North Carolina Press. '80.

Collins, J.M. U.S.-Soviet military balance: concepts and capabilities, 1960–1980. McGraw-Hill. '80.

Congressional Quarterly, Inc. U.S. defense policy; weapons, strategy and commitments, 2nd ed. Congressional Quarterly. 1414 22nd St. N.W. Washington, D.C. 20037. '80.

Dagget, Stephen. What you need to know about the new generation of nuclear weapons. Institute for Policy Studies. 1901 Q St. N.W. Washington, D.C. 20009. '80.

Fallows, J.M. National defense. Random House. '81.

Foreign Policy Association. SALT II: toward security or danger. Foreign Policy Association. 205 Lexington Ave. New York, N.Y. 10016. '79.

Foreign Policy Research Institute. The three per cent solution and the future of NATO. Foreign Policy Research Institute. 3508 Market St. Philadelphia, Pa. 19104. '81.

Gansler, J.S. The defense industry. Massachusetts Institute of Technology Press. '80.

Gervasi, Tom. Arsenal of democracy II. American military power in the 1980s and the origins of the new cold war; with a survey of American weapons and arms exports. Grove Press. '81.

Gilpin, Robert. War and change in world politics. Cambridge University Press. '81.

Huisken, Ronald. The origin of the strategic cruise missile. Praeger. '81.

International Institute for Strategic Studies. The military balance 1980–81. Facts on File, Inc. '80.

International Institute for Strategic Studies. Strategic survey 1980. IISS. 23 Tavistock St. London WC2E 7NQ. '81.

Jordan, A.A. and W.J. Taylor, Jr. American national security: policy and process. Johns Hopkins University Press. '81.

Kaiser, Karl, Lord, Winston, Montbrial, Thierry de, and Watt, David. Western security. What has changed? What should be

done? Council on Foreign Relations. 58 E
York, N.Y., 10021. '81.

Kaldor, Mary. The baroque arsenal. Hill and W

Karsten, Peter, ed. The military in America. Fr

Keliher, J.G. The negotiations for mutual and
ductions: the search for arms control in c
gamon Press. '80.

Kinnard, Douglas. The secretary of defense
tucky Press. '81.

Kojm, C.A. and the Editors of the Foreig
The ABC's of defense: America's m
(Headline Series) Foreign Policy Assoc

Lehman, J.F. and Weiss, Seymour. Beyon
Praeger. '81.

Long, Franklin and Reppy, Judith, eds. Th
ons: decision making for military R&

Millar, T. B. The east-west strategic bal
'81.

Pechman, J.A., ed. Setting national pri
Brookings Institution. '81.

Potter, William C., ed. Verification an
strategic deception. Westview Pre

Record, Jeffrey. The rapid deployment
tervention in the Persian Gulf. I
Analysis. 675 Massachusetts Ave.

Scoville, Herbert. MX: prescription fo
stitute of Technology Press. '81.

Sivard, R.L. World military and
Priorities. Box 1003, Leesburg,

Stockholm International Peace Re
ments and disarmament yearb
Technology Press. '81.

Thompson, W.S., ed. National sec
ness to strength. Institute fo
811, 260 California St. San F

United States Congress. Congre
for defense: a review of key
Supt. of Docs. Washington

United States Congress. Strateg
ological warfare. Sub-com
and Scientific Affairs and
mittee on Foreign Affairs
session. Supt. of Docs. W

AEI
    I
    A
    1
AEI F
    ha
    Cl
Arms C
    A.
    cle
Atlantic
    Fal
Atlantic
    Fall
Aviation
    cites
Aviation
    chie
Aviation
    Defe
Bulletin o
    ruble
Bulletin of
    weapo
Bulletin of
    fense l
Business W
    the U.

Business Week. p 102–3. N. 24, '80. Risks in Reagan's strategic military planning.

Business Week. p 110+. Je. 8, '81. Absorbing a defense buildup?

*Business Week. p 171–80. Jl. 20, '81. Building a navy to rule the seas again.

The Christian Science Monitor, p 12–3. Ag. 26, '80. Deterring nuclear war: the new dangers. Elizabeth Pond.

The Christian Science Monitor. p 12–13. Je. 19, '81. The state of the alliance: the missile-watch. Elizabeth Pond.

*The Christian Science Monitor. p 22. Ag. 12, '81. America needs small carriers. Stansfield Turner.

Commentary. 69:31–8. My. '80. ABM question. Carnes Lord.

Commentary. 70:28–32. Ag. '80. How to pay for survival. Herbert Stein.

Commentary. 70:27–34. S. '80. New arms race? E.N. Luttwak.

Daedalus: Journal of the American Academy of Arts and Sciences. 109:4. Fall 1980. U.S. defense policy in the 1980s.

Daedalus: Journal of the American Academy of Arts and Sciences. 110:1. Winter 1981. U.S. defense policy in the 1980s.

The Defense Monitor. 10:3 '81. Military budget up $80 billion in two years. The Center for Defense Information. 122 Maryland Ave. N.E. Washington, D.C. 20002

*The Department of State Bulletin. 80:63–67. My. '80. Protecting U.S. interests in the Persian Gulf region. Harold Brown.

*The Department of State Bulletin. 80:27 N. '80. Essentials of security: arms and more. E.S. Muskie.

Department of State Bulletin. 80:35–6. N. '80 America's strength: ideals and military power. E.S. Muskie.

The Department of State Bulletin. 80:6. D. '80. SALT and the future of arms control. E.S. Muskie.

*The Department of State Bulletin. 80:46+. Jl. '81. Requirements of our defense policy. C.W. Weinberger.

The Department of State Bulletin. 80:51+. Jl. '81. Arms transfers and the national interest. J.L. Buckley.

*The Department of State Bulletin. 80:31–34. Ag. '81. Arms control for the 1980s: an American policy. A.M. Haig.

*The Department of State Bulletin. 81:10–13. D. '81. U.S. program for peace and arms control. Ronald Reagan.

East-West Outlook. 4:1+. (Jl./Ag. '81) George Kennan proposes 50 percent reduction in U.S. and Soviet nuclear arsenals. American Committee on East-West Accord. 227 Massachusetts Ave. N.E. Suite 300. Washington, D.C. 20002.

Economist. 279:54+. Je. 6, '81. Defending the gulf; a survey.

*Forbes. 125:37–9. My. 26, '80. Critical view of the U.S. military
    establishment. E.N. Luttwak.

Forbes. 126:57–62. Jl. 21, '80. Age of aircraft carrier diplomacy. A.
    Hughey.

Forbes 126:44. S. 1, '80. For want of a nail . . . Beth Brophy.

Forbes. 126:49–50+. S. 15, '80. Great push-button delusion. S.N.
    Chakravarty.

Forbes. 126:133–4+. O. 13, '80. Our weakened defenses—money
    alone is not the answer. B.M. Blechman and L. H. Gelb.

Forbes. 127:38+. Je. 8, '81. Flight of the Harrier. Beth Brophy.

*Foreign Affairs. 59:102–125. Fall '80. Do negotiated arms limita-
    tions have a future? B.M. Blechman.

Foreign Affairs. 59:352–365. Winter '80/'81. Rethinking arms
    control. Christoph Bertram.

Foreign Affairs. 60:17–34. Fall '81. Making the all-volunteer force
    work: a national service approach. C.C. Moskos.

Foreign Affairs. 60:287–304. Winter '81/'82. MAD vs. NUTS: the
    mutual hostage relationship of the super-powers. S.M. Keeny,
    Jr. and W.K.H. Panofsky.

Foreign Affairs. 60:305–26. Winter '81/'82. The implications of
    theater nuclear weapons in Europe. Christoph Bertram.

Foreign Affairs. 60:327–46. Winter '81/'82. NATO and nuclear
    weapons: reasons and unreason. Stanley Hoffmann.

Foreign Policy. 39:14–27. Summer '80. Victory is possible. C.S.
    Gray and K. Payne.

Foreign Policy. 39:28–39. Summer '80. Doing nothing. E.C. Ra-
    venal.

Foreign Policy 40:99–118. Fall '80. Overarming and underwhelm-
    ing. R.B. Posen and S.W. Van Evera.

Foreign Policy. 41:82–94. Winter '80–'81. The TNF tangle. R.L.
    Garthoff.

*Foreign Policy. 43:17–32. Summer '81. America engulfed. D.D.
    Newsom.

Foreign Policy. 44:82–93. Fall '81. Quota testing. P.D. Zimmer-
    man.

Foreign Policy. 44:94–106. Fall '81. Space wars. D.A. Andelman.

Fortune. 102:38–44. S. 8, '80. Mental gap in the defense debate.
    William Guzzardi, Jr.

*Fortune. 103:52–58. Ja. 26, '81. A defense budget for the 1980s.
    D.D. Holt.

Fortune. 103:79–80+. My. 18, '81. Cap Weinberger's Pentagon
    revolution. D.D. Holt.

Harper's. 262:20+. Ja. '81. Resource wars. M.T. Klare.

Nation. 230:417+. Ap. 12, '80. ABM—the end of deterrence. Alan Wolfe.

Nation. 232:67–93. Ja. 24, '81. Letter to America. E.P. Thompson.

The New Republic. 182:20–3. Ap. 26, '80. Solving the defense riddle. S.L. Canby.

The New Republic. 183:7–9. Ag. 30, '80. Target practice. [Presidential directive 59] John Osborne.

The New Republic. 184:11–13. Ja. 24, '81. Defense without mirrors. M.M. Kondracke.

The New Republic. 184:16+. My. 16, '81. Armed for inflation. Ronald Steel.

New York. 14:14+. Ap. 6, '81. Bullet bites back. [defense and inflation] Jack Egan.

New York. 14:18–25. Je. 22, '81. $1.5 trillion for defense? M. Kramer.

The New York Review of Books. p 40+. N. 20, '80. The myth of missile accuracy. Andrew Cockburn and Alexander Cockburn.

The New York Review of Books. 28:3+. My. 14, '81. How to wreck the economy. Lester Thurow.

The New York Review of Books. pp 26–31. D. 17, '81. The trap of rearmament. J.M. Fallows.

The New York Times. A1+. S. 22, '80. Nuclear gains by Russians prompt a reaction by U.S. Richard Burt.

The New York Times. A1+. S. 24, '80. Questions raised on the readiness of the army for a protracted conflict. M.W. Browne.

The New York Times. A1. S. 25, '80. Amid shortages, navy maintains edge over Soviet. Drew Middleton.

The New York Times. E5. O. 12, '80. A debate: are U.S. defenses ready, rusty or adequate? D.L. Aaron, W.R. Van Cleave, Alton Frye and Richard Burt.

The New York Times. D2. O. 15, '80. Arms budget's heavy impact. A.S. Eichner.

The New York Times. A1+. D. 7, '80. Moscow's arms buildup a major issue for Reagan. Richard Burt.

The New York Times. C1+. Ja. 11, '81. Why defense costs so much. Richard Halloran.

*The New York Times. C3. F. 1, '81. We spend too much on defense. G.R. LaRocque.

The New York Times. C3. My. 17, '81. No great threat from military spending. William Nordhaus.

The New York Times. D2. S. 4, '81. Wall St. brake on the military. Leonard Silk.

The New York Times. C1+. S. '13, '81. Now it's defense vs. the
    deficit. Richard Halloran.
The New York Times. A1. S. 24, '81. New cuts to claim missiles,
    warships and army division. Richard Halloran.
The New York Times. A1+. O. 3, '81. Reagan drops mobile MX
    plan, urges basing missiles in silos; proposes building B-1
    bomber. Richard Halloran.
°The New York Times. D1. O. 4, '81. Vulnerability assumes the
    Soviets will strike first. L.H. Gelb.
°The New York Times. D5. O. 11, '81. At 'a minimum $200 million
    a bird,' B-1 bomber debate begins. Richard Halloran.
The New York Times Magazine. 14–17+. My. 10, '81. Toward a
    new defense strategy. Stansfield Turner.
The New York Times Magazine. 24–27+. N. 1, '81. How many bil-
    lions for defense? Hedrick Smith.
Newsweek. 95:38–9. Je. 16, '80. America's thin blue line. B. Came.
Newsweek. 96:30–36. Jl. 14, '80. Defending the oil fields; the U.S.
    military buildup.
Newsweek. 96:74. S. 29, '80. Draft isn't the issue. Milton Fried-
    man.
Newsweek. 96:48+. O. 27, '80. Is America strong enough?
Newsweek. 96:73. N. 24, '80. Rapid Deployment Force lifts off for
    Egypt. A. Deming and others.
Newsweek. 97:22. Ja. 19, '81. Defense: the hard choices. M. Beck
    and D.C. Martin.
Newsweek. 97:98. Je. 1, '81. Throwing money at defense. Meg
    Greenfield.
Newsweek. 97:28+. Je. 8, '81. Reagan's defense buildup. Does it
    make sense. Can we afford it?
Newsweek. 98:32–39. O. 5, '81. The nuclear arms race.
Orbis. 24:511–32. Fall '80. U.S. general-purpose forces: four essen-
    tial reforms. A.N. Sabrosky.
Progressive. 45:18–20+. F. '81. Army in search of a war. M.T.
    Klare.
Science. 211:681–3. F. 13, '81. William Perry and the weapons
    gamble. E. Marshall.
Science. 212:1006. My. 29, '81. DOD announces weapons buying
    reforms.
Scientific American. 244:31–41. F. '81. Advances in anti-subma-
    rine warfare. J.S. Wit.
Society. 17:56–60 Jl./Ag. '80. Executive and the joint chiefs. L.J.
    Korb.
Time. 115:24–7+. Je. 9, '80. Who'll fight for America?
Time. 118:6+. Jl. 27, '81. How to spend a trillion.

*USA Today. 110:18–21. Jl. '81. Limits of military power for national security. Seymour Melman.

U.S. News & World Report. 89:60–1. S. 8, '80. "Can't miss" weapons—revolution in warfare. W.J. Perry.

U.S. News & World Report. 89:38. S. 22, '80. A firsthand look at what ails the navy. Orr Kelly.

U.S. News & World Report. 90:27–29. Ja. 26, '81. From Carterites: parting advice on national security.

U.S. News & World Report. 90:44–6. Ap. 13, '81. What's being done about waste in the Pentagon. C.W. Weinberger.

U.S. News & World Report. 90:35–7. My. 4, '81. Battleships: again a center of strife.

Vital Speeches of the Day. 47:66–71. N. 15, '80. United States Armed Forces today. Harold Brown.

The Wall Street Journal. p 34. O. 23, '80. The defense budget shell game. J.R. Schlesinger.

The Wall Street Journal. p 1+. O. 30, '80. Big carrier illustrates manpower difficulties afflicting U.S. forces. W.S. Mossberg.

The Wall Street Journal. p 26. Ja. 21, '81. Hard choices on defense spending begin now. W.S. Mossberg.

*The Wall Street Journal. p 20. Ja. 23, '81. The case for military reform. Gary Hart.

The Wall Street Journal. p 1+. Ap. 20, '81. Costly new M1 tank fails more army tests; price keeps increasing. W.S. Mossberg.

The Wall Street Journal. p 1+. Je. 1, '81. Many air force planes often can't be flown for lack of spare parts. W.S. Mossberg.

The Wall Street Journal. p 1+. Ag. 21, '81. In military buildup, big contractors face supplier bottlenecks. G.F. Seib and R J Harris Jr.

The Wall Street Journal. p 1+. S. 9, '81. Reagan campaign plan for rearming America hits budget realities. W.S. Mossberg.

The Wall Street Journal. p 1+. D. 22, '81. The cruise missile and an old romance revive the battleship. J.M. Perry.

The Washington Post. A2. My. 20, '80. Allied defense costs: an unequal sharing of the burden. Michael Getler.

The Washington Post. A1. Ag. 27, '80. Sailors quit over low pay, loneliness. Mike Sager.

The Washington Post. A17. N. 19, '80. Not a binge, but a buildup. Melvin Laird.

The Washington Post. A24. D. 19, '80. Soviets can kill 50 percent of U.S. land missiles, expert says. G.C. Wilson.

The Washington Post. A13. Ja. 16, '81. Pentagon outlay presents Reagan with dilemma. G.C. Wilson.

The Washington Post. A2. Ja. 26, '81. U.S. ability to retaliate after
    nuclear attack concerns officials. Michael Getler.
*The Washington Post. C1 and C5. F. 22, '81. Are our weapons
    too complex? Not if you compare them to the Russians'. G.C.
    Wilson and W.J. Perry.
*The Washington Post. A1+. Ap. 25, '81. Reagan's defense spend-
    ing could turn into economic nightmare. R.G. Kaiser.
The Washington Post. A1 and A5. Je. 7, '81. Persian gulf commit-
    ment hastily improvised, ex-official says. Don Oberdorfer.
The Washington Post. A1+. N. 15, '81. The war game: Europe and
    the bomb. Bradley Graham.
The Washington Post. A1+. N. 16, '81. The war game: battlefield
    Europe. Walter Pincus and Bradley Graham.
The Washington Post. A1+. N. 17, '81. The war game: Europe's
    nuclear pacifists. Leonard Downie Jr.
The Washington Post. A1+. N. 18, '81. The war game: birth of a
    Euromissile. Walter Pincus.
The Washington Post. A1+. N. 19, '81. The war game: island arse-
    nal. Leonard Downie Jr.
*The White House. Press release. Background statement by the
    White House on programs for the B-1 bomber and MX mis-
    sile. O. 2, '81.
World Press Review. 27:53. N. '80. New nuclear strategy. K. Su-
    brahmanyam.
World Press Review. 28:24–6. Ag. '81. Protecting the Gulf's oil.
    R. Harvey.
World Press Review. 28:39–44. N. '81. The new arms debate.